September–December 2021

Day by Day
with
God

Rooting women's lives in the Bible

The Bible Reading Fellowship
15 The Chambers, Vineyard
Abingdon OX14 3FE
brf.org.uk

The Bible Reading Fellowship (BRF) is a Registered Charity (233280)

ISBN 978 1 80039 016 4
All rights reserved

Distributed in Australia by:
MediaCom Education Inc, PO Box 610, Unley, SA 5061
Tel: 1 800 811 311 | admin@mediacom.org.au

Distributed in New Zealand by:
Scripture Union Wholesale, PO Box 760, Wellington
Tel: 04 385 0421 | suwholesale@clear.net.nz

Acknowledgements

Scripture quotations marked with the following abbreviations are taken from the version shown. Where no abbreviation is given, the quotation is taken from the same version as the headline reference. NIV: The Holy Bible, New International Version (Anglicised edition) copyright © 1979, 1984, 2011 by Biblica. Used by permission of Hodder & Stoughton Publishers, a Hachette UK company. All rights reserved. 'NIV' is a registered trademark of Biblica. UK trademark number 1448790. NLT: The Holy Bible, New Living Translation, copyright © 1996, 2004, 2007, 2013. Used by permission of Tyndale House Publishers, Inc., Carol Stream, Illinois 60188. All rights reserved. CEV: The Contemporary English Version. New Testament © American Bible Society 1991, 1992, 1995. Old Testament © American Bible Society 1995. Anglicisations © British & Foreign Bible Society 1996. Used by permission. AMP: The Amplified® Bible (AMP), Copyright © 2015 by The Lockman Foundation. Used by permission. www.Lockman.org. NRSV: The New Revised Standard Version of the Bible, Anglicised edition, copyright © 1989, 1995 by the Division of Christian Education of the National Council of the Churches of Christ in the United States of America. Used by permission. All rights reserved. ESV: The Holy Bible, English Standard Version, published by HarperCollins Publishers, © 2001 Crossway Bibles, a division of Good News Publishers. Used by permission. All rights reserved. TPT: The Passion Translation®. Copyright © 2017, 2018 by Passion & Fire Ministries, Inc. Used by permission. All rights reserved. ThePassionTranslation. com. MSG: *The Message*, copyright © 1993, 1994, 1995, 1996, 2000, 2001, 2002 by Eugene H. Peterson. Used by permission of NavPress. All rights reserved. Represented by Tyndale House Publishers, Inc.

A catalogue record for this book is available from the British Library

Printed and bound by Gutenberg Press, Tarxien, Malta

Day by Day with God

Edited by **Jackie Harris**

September–December 2021

Writers in this issue

Chine McDonald is head of community fundraising and public engagement at Christian Aid. A regular contributor to BBC Religion & Ethics programmes, she also sits on a number of charity boards, including Christians Against Poverty, Greenbelt Festival and the Church & Media Network.

Sara Batts-Neale is a priest in the diocese of Chelmsford. She is currently the Anglican chaplain to the University of Essex. Married to Tim, they live with a dog and host a cat.

Rosemary Green has four adult children and 14 grandchildren. She lives in Abingdon where she is involved in ministry among seniors in her local church, including a large group for those who have been bereaved.

Alianore Smith is church partnership manager at International Justice Mission. Previously known as Nell Goddard, Alianore is recently married and the author of *Musings of a Clergy Child* (BRF, 2017).

Bridget Plass is a writer and speaker, appearing and touring all over the world. For the last ten years, she has enjoyed being actively involved in the programme at Scargill House in Yorkshire and absolutely loves living near Durham.

Hannah Fytche read theology at Cambridge University. She is passionate about seeing God's love transform lives and communities, and embraces this passion through writing, speaking and spending time with friends and family.

Anne Le Tissier is an author, preacher and speaker, called and impassioned to disciple others in their ongoing walk with God. She enjoys the country life, sharing quality time over meals with friends and chatting to her chickens.

Fiona Barnard is a TEFL/ESOL teacher and staff member of Friends International. She works with international students, encouraging local Christians to reach out in friendship and evangelism to make disciples.

Sheila Jacobs is a writer, an editor and an award-winning author. She attends an Elim church, where she serves on the pastoral care team, and is a day chaplain at a retreat centre. Her passion is helping others meet with Jesus.

Maxine Hallett struggled with drug dependency for 25 years. She became a Christian five years ago and now works at Tonbridge Baptist Church running the senior work. She writes devotions about walking with God in the outdoors for an online community page.

Welcome

Amid the challenges and turbulence of recent times, isn't it wonderful to know that in our ever-changing lives and world there is one constant: our unchanging God? And not only does he never change, but he also never grows faint or weary (Isaiah 40:28) and is never taken by surprise.

He knows the challenges we're facing, the hopes we cherish, the secret sadness we hide and the desires of our hearts. And as we come to him in his word, we are assured of his strength, his promises, his comfort and his guidance.

It has been so encouraging to hear from readers who have written to tell us how different notes have spoken into their situation or inspired them, and we pray that this issue, too, will bring God's word alive to you.

We begin with something a little different, as our contributors each share a verse or passage that means a lot to them. Isn't it amazing how God guides us to a scripture just when we need it? I wonder if any of your favourites are there.

We end with a new contributor – Maxine Hallett – who has worked with Jennifer Rees Larcombe and loves to encourage others in their faith. Maxine shares a little of her testimony before drawing the year to a close with a study of Psalm 30.

In between, we are thinking about how we can honour God with our bodies, delving into the book of Micah, learning from Gideon, being challenged about our attitude to money and studying some of the stories Jesus told. As we move towards the season of Advent and through to Christmas, we focus on the image of light, find inspiration from Mary's song of praise, keep company with Elizabeth and Zechariah and explore God's promises to those who wait.

The evenings may be drawing in and the sunshine giving way to chilly winds, but we're praying that God's Spirit will warm your hearts as you follow these readings through the autumn and winter months, and remind you that he is with you in your walk of faith.

Let us pray for one another as we draw close to the one who loves us and receive strength from him.

Jackie Harris, Editor

A feast of good things

Jackie Harris writes:

Before we fell in love with the Scandinavian concept of hygge (cosiness, comfort, conviviality and wellness) there was the smorgasbord, a collection of hot and cold dishes served together which originated in Sweden. It has largely become just another word for a buffet meal, but it is more than simply a collection of dishes. The essence of a real smorgasbord is all about taking your time to eat and to talk to your guests as you graze through a wonderfully laid-out table.

It's an image I had in mind as I commissioned this first study, for the Bible is often described as food for the soul. 'When your words came, I ate them; they were my joy and my heart's delight,' says Jeremiah (15:16, NIV). Ezekiel, too, was given God's word to eat (Ezekiel 2:8—3:3) and, like the psalmist, declared it 'sweeter than honey' (Psalm 119:103, NIV).

And Jesus himself spoke of the importance of drawing nourishment from God's word when he was tempted in the desert: 'Man shall not live on bread alone, but on every word that comes from the mouth of God' (Matthew 4:4, NIV).

Reading and studying God's word is vital if we are to grow in our faith. I love the NLT version of 2 Timothy 3:16–17: 'All Scripture is inspired by God and is useful to teach us what is true… It corrects us when we are wrong and teaches us to do what is right. God uses it to prepare and equip his people to do every good work.'

Over the next few days, we will be studying a variety of scriptures which each mean something special to this issue's contributors. There is a mix of Old and New Testament readings, single verses and whole passages, familiar and perhaps less well read. Some are words of comfort and encouragement; others challenge us or call us to action.

As you come to read them, imagine a table laid before you full of good things. You are invited to dine with the Holy Spirit, so make yourself comfortable, slow down and savour each word. What does God want to share with you as you read and what do you want to say to him in response? Bon appétit!

Don't look back

As soon as they had brought them out, one of them said, 'Flee for your lives! Don't look back…' But Lot's wife looked back, and she became a pillar of salt. (NIV)

I was back home in Guernsey to care for my poorly mother but popping out for daily exercise. After one particular clifftop walk, I looked back for a final glimpse of the familiar beauty, which pulled at my heart for a life that could have been if I hadn't moved away. But then some words came to mind with profound clarity: *Stop looking back at where you have been and concentrate on where you are going.* Later, while prayerfully mulling over this, another phrase nudged me – 'Remember Lot's wife!' (Luke 17:32) – prompting me to reread her story.

The Holy Spirit was convicting me of my discontent, arising from my looking back at what was – or could have been – instead of staying focused on God's presence in my present. It was a disgruntlement I was allowing to fester while distracted with fond memories of that cherished place, and I had to make a choice: stop looking back or, spiritually speaking, turn into a lifeless pillar of salt!

Life will inevitably change. We may suffer a decline in health, income or comfort, lose an identity, role or partner, etc. But Jesus urges us to keep our hearts focused on the tasks of today, leaning into his presence through prayer and the word. When we do that, his promises become our reality and not just words on a page; peace and well-being, wisdom and guidance, provision for our needs, equipping for purpose…

It is good to be grateful for the gifts of yesterday, but if they unsettle our contentment in God, holding us back from delighting in him and yielding to his will, then looking back is risky. Life may have changed, but God with us remains the same – and God's presence is an unchanging reality that we can enjoy for eternity.

Father, I name before you the root of my discontent with the life you have blessed me with today. I still my thoughts and emotions, to focus on your presence, your promises and your ongoing purpose. Amen

ANNE LE TISSIER

God is in control

Job replied to the Lord: 'I know that you can do all things; no purpose of yours can be thwarted.' (NIV)

Forty years ago, I was in a mess. Angry and depressed, everything seemed to be crashing around me. I thought the book of Job would speak to me. His life had crashed around him, too.

I found much of the book confusing. I wasn't sure what was truth and what was half-truth as Job and his three friends talked – they in their smug accusations, he in his self-righteous defence. Finally, they had no more to say, and the young man Elihu, hitherto silent, told Job to stop talking and listen to God. God spoke of his wisdom, his existence from eternity, his creation of the world and everything in it. Job was humbled.

When I reached chapter 42, it was as if God took his highlighting pen to my Bible (a rare experience for me), as Job affirms, 'I know that you can do all things; no purpose of yours can be thwarted.' I saw that God really is sovereign, all-wise, all-powerful, all-loving. And he makes no mistakes.

There is no point in trusting a God who is right only 98% of the time; he has to be 100%, yes 110%. As I read those verses in Job, God seemed to take a huge mallet and knock a 25-cm-diameter post solidly into the ground, a post I can clutch tightly. That conviction has remained with me ever since.

There are still times when, like Peter stepping out of the boat to walk on the water, I look at the 'waves' of the difficulties around me and fear takes over. I have to choose whether to focus on the waves of uncertainty or whether to pray, with Peter, 'Lord, save me.' The situation may not change, but my attitude does, and I find renewed joy and freedom as I choose to trust the all-reliable God.

Lord, thank you for the confidence that you really are in control of matters large and small, in world events and in personal details. Thank you that I can trust you and your good purposes, even when I don't understand. Amen

ROSEMARY GREEN

Quiet blessings

'Be still, and know that I am God.' (NIV)

Like many people, I live life at a hectic pace. The nature of my work often means tight deadlines. I live alone, so I like to meet up with friends as much as I can. I love being involved in a retreat house as a day chaplain and leading retreats and, of course, there's church and house group, as well as maintaining a house and large garden.

When we found ourselves in weeks of social isolation due to the coronavirus outbreak, I began to feel a creeping anxiety. It reminded me very much of the years I suffered from agoraphobia, not able to get out, not free. During that time, I turned to and relied on God in a very real way. It was only when I was once again in enforced solitude that I realised I had started to drift away from that close relationship when I became well. In effect, I'd started to 'do Christian life' without actually connecting with Jesus much of the time.

The tracts of time alone were difficult but presented an opportunity to regain that stillness so that I could know his presence again. So much of our relationship with God is about being still before him. Following that comes the knowing – who he is; understanding that he is the 'I am'; and there is no one and nothing else we can truly rely on.

It surprised me to discover how much I'd been building my life on sinking sand, when all that really matters is being close to the one who isn't surprised by the magnitude of life's ups and downs. Being still leads to peace, faith and confidence in the one who holds the future.

Be still. Can you discern God's presence? He is the 'I am' – always present. In the quietness, praise him, out loud or in your heart.

SHEILA JACOBS

God's longing for us

'What can I do with you?… Your love is like the morning mist, like the early dew that disappears.' (NIV)

Hosea is a prophetic, poetic Old Testament book. Through his prophet, God speaks to his wayward creation with great anger – and with even greater love.

His people's love is like ephemeral morning mist, we read. We experience this too, for *we* are God's people. Our devotion is like dew that is burned up quickly, gone before noon. We find it hard, I think, faithfully to return to God each day, especially when times are tough.

Yet despite our fickle devotion, we are dearly loved. God asks throughout Hosea: 'What can I do with you?' Because his love for us is faithful, he longs to help us live in a way that rings true with the opening words of Hosea 6: 'Let us return to the Lord.'

I first read Hosea when I was 15, sitting in an empty dorm room at summer camp. I can't put this experience into words – my heart simply, undeniably burned within me (to borrow Luke's phrase) at this message of God's anger and love.

This complicated poem of God's feelings towards his people opened my eyes to his heartbreak; it showed me that God yearns for me to know him, and that it – incredibly – pains him when I damage my life by turning from him.

It showed me that I needed to learn to receive Christ's strong and precious grace. Without God forgiving and sustaining me, my devotion will always be like morning mist. Yet Christ Jesus is the brilliant answer to God's question: what God can do with us is help us – not because of our merit, but because of his love – by coming to live, die and rise among us.

This means that the opening words of Hosea 6 can finally ring true: we *can* return to the Lord, whose appearing is as sure as the sunrise.

Listen to God's love and longing for you. Read Hosea 6:4, replacing 'Ephraim' and 'Judah' with your own name: 'What can I do with you…?' Pray: Thank you, Jesus, that you make a way for us to return to God. Amen

HANNAH FYTCHE

Amazing God

Your thoughts are far beyond my understanding, much more than I could ever imagine. I try to count your thoughts, but they outnumber the grains of sand on the beach. And when I awake, I will find you nearby. (CEV)

The whole of this psalm is a favourite for many of us. The idea of God knitting me has always charmed me! So why these few verses? Because to me they sum up the God I believe in.

As a child, attending a Catholic primary school, I loved the chapel. The colours and the smell of incense opened a window to a world belonging to someone distant, mysterious and rather frightening. What a relief to later be introduced to an approachable Father God.

However, I began to feel that the constant emphasis on the familiarity of God suggested he was almost on our level, passing the marmalade over the breakfast table, chatting about the weather, saying yes to our every small request. No mystery. No mighty power. No wonder many of us became disappointed that our requests appeared to be ignored and felt rejected!

David had a very special relationship with God. Growing up as a boy shepherd and later on the run from Saul, he lived amid danger for much of his life, but discovered a mighty protector God under whose wings he would be safe.

His psalms show how tuned-in he was to the vagaries of weather, the danger and beauty of the night, the wildness of the mountains, the wonder of water. His was a truly awesome God, but also a protective parent who loved him and watched over him. Can we, too, hold this balance? Can we believe in a God so powerful and omniscient his thoughts outnumber the grains of sand on the beach, and yet so loving and caring he will be there every morning, waiting for each one of his children to wake up so together we can face the day?

Dear Father, today help me to reflect on the many extraordinary aspects of your character and hold you in balance as David did. Amen

BRIDGET PLASS

With God we can flourish

'I am the true Vine, and My Father is the vinedresser. Every branch in Me that does not bear fruit, He takes away; and every *branch* that continues to bear fruit, He [repeatedly] prunes, so that it will bear more fruit [even richer and finer fruit].' (AMP)

Walking along a cycle path next to a busy, polluted and noisy motorway, I was surprised to see a line of cherry trees with huge ripe cherries. I thought that the pollution from the traffic would have hindered their growth in some way, but the fruit looked delicious, vibrant in colour and very edible. It was not an ideal location for these trees – no doubt they had been planted years ago – but their branches bowed with luscious fruit.

Looking at them, I was reminded of these verses in John's gospel, which have always encouraged me. They teach us that it does not matter to God that we have been polluted with toxins from our past. As long as we stay connected to him through prayer and studying his word, he will enable us to blossom, flourish and produce the fruit of the Spirit that Paul talks about in Galatians (5:22–23). What a wonderful promise!

Of course, Jesus indicates that this might involve some pruning in our lives of old habits and attitudes, but the 'fruits' we will experience – and others will see in us – are love, joy, peace, patience, kindness, goodness, faithfulness, gentleness and self-control.

When we remain in Jesus, we are given hope and the promise that we will change. It may take years, but God is at work in our lives, enabling us to become the best version of ourselves.

Why not take a walk with God and look for fruit trees and wild berries growing in the hedgerows? Then praise the Lord for all the pruning that he has done and is doing in your life.

MAXINE HALLETT

The folded grave clothes

Simon Peter arrived and went inside. He also noticed the linen wrappings lying there, while the cloth that had covered Jesus' head was folded up and lying apart from the other wrappings. Then the [other] disciple… saw and believed. (NLT)

It was 4.00 pm on Easter Sunday. I still could not write the sermon for a baptism in two hours. Panic was rising as I pictured a church full of celebrating friends and family on a day of such significance. I had nothing to say. My mind was too full of grief.

My father had died just a month before and I was going through my parents' correspondence. I had found a letter written to my 13-year-old mother by her mother. It was a 'when you read this, I'll be dead' note full of love, full of sadness, full of advice. I wept and wept at the cruelty of death, the enormity of my mother's loss, the pointlessness of it all. Meanwhile, the non-sermon loomed. 'Lord,' I cried, holding the folded letter before him, 'you have got to do something!'

'Folded.' The folded page triggered a memory of the word 'folded' in the resurrection story. When the disciples looked into the empty grave, they saw a folded cloth which had been around Jesus' head. It struck me as odd that amid the energy and excitement of the resurrection, either Jesus or the angels should pause to fold some material, all neat and tidy: why? Then it hit me. It was because Jesus no longer needed it. He was alive.

I stared at the folded letter. 'It is folded because it is not required,' Jesus seemed to whisper. 'The grief of your mother and grandmother is done. Their separation is over. They are together now with me.' Resurrection suddenly was so much more real. The truth of it touched me where it never had before. In the light of a glorious eternity, a new perspective on decades of pain emerged. And I was comforted. (Enough to write that sermon, and beyond that, to process my bereavement.)

How has the Lord brought comfort to your heart? Remember and savour his tender love.

FIONA BARNARD

Trust in God's strength

'The Lord will fight for you; you need only to be still.' (NIV)

I am one of those people who likes to keep myself extremely busy. I am excited by too many opportunities and find it very difficult to say no. At times I have found that my busyness has tipped over into chaos and I am teetering on the edge of burnout. Sometimes the work seems overwhelming, the to-do lists never-ending, and I feel like I'm trying to keep my head above the water, constantly flailing.

Sometimes the world feels overwhelming. Occasionally I have stopped listening to the news because there is so much going on in the world that causes stress and anxiety. At those times of stress, it can be tempting to either keep going without stopping or to collapse under the weight of the pressure – a place from which it feels there is no way out.

In Exodus 14, the Israelites find themselves at one of the most dramatic scenes in the whole Bible. After God has freed them from the Egyptians and led them – a pillar of cloud by day, and fire by night – right to the Red Sea, Pharaoh and his army are gaining and threatening to catch up with them. Of course, they are terrified. With the Red Sea in front of them and Pharaoh right behind, it feels like their grand escape will not have its happy ending.

They then cry out to Moses, doubting God's provision for them, asking so many fear-filled questions. And Moses says these astounding words that I often think about when I feel overwhelmed and afraid: 'The Lord will fight for you; you need only to be still.' It is so releasing to trust in God's strength rather than our own. Because we all know the end of this story.

Lord God, thank you for fighting for us. Help us to be still and trust in you. Amen

CHINE MCDONALD

Don't worry!

'[Don't] worry about everyday life… Look at the birds. They don't plant or harvest or store food in barns, for your heavenly Father feeds them. And aren't you far more valuable to him than they are?' (NLT)

I think the instruction not to worry is one of the most repeated in the Bible. Certainly I have a number of verses on this theme underlined, but this one kept popping into my head when I was sitting at home following my redundancy and wondering what to do next.

Perhaps it was the regular visitors to our garden which I began to notice and look forward to seeing. A pair of blackbirds appeared both morning and evening and seemed to find plenty of treats on our lawn. A little group of sparrows took it in turns to enjoy a splash around in the bird bath, and a couple of magpies would swoop in for a stroll around and a drink. One of them had only one leg and struggled to balance as she stooped down to pick something off the lawn. She persevered, though, sitting down for short breaks before trying again. Two rather portly pigeons also seemed to make themselves at home, soaking their feet in the bird bath when it was hot and clearing up the bird seed which the sparrows let fall from the feeder.

These feathered friends not only kept me entertained, but also led me to this passage, which speaks of God's care and provision for us. As I reflected on it, I was reminded of how God had cared and provided for me in the past. Surely he would do so again.

But Jesus is offering more than words of comfort. He encourages his listeners not only to trust in God's provision, but also to focus on God's priorities. There is always work to be done for him. I am slowly learning that shifting our attention from ourselves to his goodness and purposes is the best antidote to worry.

Father, thank you for the many lessons you teach us through your creation and for your assurance that you care for us and will provide for us. Help us to trust you more and to have an eternal perspective. Amen

JACKIE HARRIS

Finding the best fit for our life

'You did not choose me but I chose you. And I appointed you to go and bear fruit, fruit that will last, so that the Father will give you whatever you ask him in my name.' (NRSV)

In the chapel at Westcott House, the theological college where I trained, an icon sits to the right of the altar. Illuminated by a candle, Christ is depicted holding an open Bible, and pointing at the text with his right hand. The text reads, 'Ye have not chosen me but I have chosen you.' I, and others, spent many hours in prayer and contemplation before this beautiful icon. I keep a card of it on my desk as I write, reminding me of those years of training and the path I have walked. So these words have just become part of me, part of my being.

Although it's a verse that is deeply helpful to a confused trainee vicar, it is not just a message for the ordained. It reminds us all that we have a calling, that we have been chosen and that we have a purpose.

But the fruit we will bear will look different for different people – and it is a mistake to judge ourselves by what others do or don't do. An apple tree produces apples – a plum tree isn't a failure if it gives a harvest of plums and not apples. It might be the fruits of the Spirit; we might learn patience, be a prophetic voice, speak in tongues. We might be great teachers. We may be natural evangelists, bringing our friends and family to know the love of God. What I do won't be the same as you.

It is so important to remember that God chose you just as much as he chose me. I believe we serve God best when we stay true to our identity as God's unique creation instead of worrying about what other people are up to. This verse reminds me daily of this truth.

Heavenly Father, I thank you that I am fearfully and wonderfully made in your image. I thank you for the person I am; created and loved by you. Amen

SARA BATTS-NEALE

Settle where God has placed you

'Also, seek the peace and prosperity of the city to which I have carried you into exile. Pray to the Lord for it, because if it prospers, you too will prosper.' (NIV)

I moved around a lot as a child. As the daughter of two vicars, I'd lived in eight houses and five cities by the time I was 16 years old.

As someone who isn't a massive fan of change, I didn't adapt particularly well to this. As a source of comfort and encouragement, people would often direct me towards Jeremiah 29:11 – a well-loved, frequently taken out of context passage. One day, however, I decided to read the whole passage, to get some perspective on God's promise.

The Israelites had been taken into exile. They did not want to be where they were. They missed their regular haunts, the places where they were known and loved. They wanted to go home.

Despite this, however, God has a simple instruction for them: 'Settle yourself where I have placed you. Put down roots. You may not want to be here. This may not have been part of your plan for your life – but I brought you here, so it is here that I will grow you.

'Get stuck in, get rooted, get engaged with the city. For if it prospers, you too will prosper. I am going to bring you home eventually, but for now, worship me here. I am the same God here as I was back home. Let me mould you and shape you and love you here. I know what I am doing.'

This passage brought me great comfort as I moved from place to place, often reluctantly. I hope it does the same for you – wherever you find yourself, whether you want to be there or not. Get stuck in. Get rooted. Get worshipping.

Father, teach me to be rooted where you have placed me. I pray for my city – may it prosper and thrive. Show me how to love it well – and remind me again that your character is unchanging, no matter where I am. Amen

ALIANORE SMITH

Honouring God with our bodies

Chine McDonald writes:

When I was studying theology at university, exploring the psychology and social sciences of religion, I came across a quote from English philosopher and physician John Locke that I think about often: 'God when he makes the prophet, does not unmake the man.' To me, this means that there is no hard line between the sacred and the profane – the sacred being those things that are otherworldly, religious and spiritual, while the profane refers to the ordinary and the physical: our jobs, our bills, our bodies.

The Locke quote was used in reference to this idea that God can work not just in some space for otherworldly things in our spirit or our soul, but also that God's work in us and his influence on our lives can be manifest in our physical bodies. This lies contrary to some of the ways in which religion has been separated from the ordinariness of life, with some Christian completely uninterested in those things deemed 'secular'. I believe that just as God can work through our hearts, so too we can use our bodies to honour God.

Over the next two weeks, we will be exploring some of the ways in which we can honour God with our bodies. With daily readings taken from throughout the Bible, we will look at the various ways the body is talked about and how it can glorify God. There are instructions to let the peace of Christ rule, to choose to put on our trainers and run the race set out before us, to flee from sexual immorality and to watch the words of our mouth.

While there are exhortations to honour God with our individual bodies, there is also the call to see ourselves as part of the body of Christ. In writing these notes, I have been encouraged and inspired to see my own body as good; to see it not as something to be denied or subjugated, but to be cared for and used for the glory of the kingdom of God. We have so many choices about what we do with our bodies. May the following days draw our minds, hearts and bodies closer to God.

Choosing a peaceful heart

Let the peace of Christ rule in your hearts, since as members of one body you were called to peace. And be thankful. (NIV)

I am a worrier, and I have discovered that many of my female friends also experience anxiety. For me, it manifests itself in dwelling on the worst possible scenario coming to pass. I find myself crippled by the helplessness I feel when facing circumstances that are far beyond my control.

Sometimes the anxiety hurts. It feels like a pain in my chest and a knot in my stomach that is difficult to untangle. I have learnt to try to manage this anxiety, to find mechanisms to gain some perspective and draw me back from the edge of panic. But what I am reminded of in today's passage is this wonderful truth that anxiety – which disrupts our peace – is not a given.

As followers of Christ who are members of a body of believers, we can choose to ask the Holy Spirit to give us a peace that passes understanding; a peace that blocks out the voices that seek to steal our joy and our trust in an almighty God. Peace is a decision – a decision to let Christ rule in our hearts and also to be thankful for it.

This is not just about us and our own well-being, but a witness to the rest of the world that we are people of peace. Our non-anxious presence in the world can move others to open their hearts to the God who stills the waters and calms the storms of our anxious hearts.

I am reminded of a quote from C.S. Lewis, which said: 'God can't give us peace and happiness apart from himself, because there is no such thing.'

God of love, may we choose peace today, no matter our circumstances. When the storms of life engulf us, may we let the peace of Christ rule in our hearts. We thank you for your never-ending grace. In Jesus' name. Amen

CHINE MCDONALD

Run the race

Therefore, since we are surrounded by such a great cloud of witnesses, let us throw off everything that hinders and the sin that so easily entangles. And let us run with perseverance the race marked out for us, fixing our eyes on Jesus, the pioneer and perfecter of faith. (NIV)

Over the past few weeks, I have put on my trainers and headed out for an early morning run. I am no Usain Bolt, but I have been finding that the discipline of getting out of the house and moving my legs, my feet stepping one in front of the other, has been great for my well-being.

I was euphoric when I eventually completed the final week of the Couch to 5k training app – a training plan that takes ordinary people from not being able to run for five minutes to comfortably running for 30 minutes non-stop.

Before I begin a run, I feel like I am not going to be able to do it. When you are in your first 30 seconds and already out of breath, 30 minutes feels very far away. But I take encouragement from the coaches on the app, whose company and motivating words make it feel doable.

The race set before us is one that needs perseverance and endurance, as we read in today's passage. It is not enough to just start the race and not complete it; what is needed is staying power. But I rejoice in the truth from this well-known passage from Hebrews, which talks about us being surrounded by a great cloud of witnesses.

The race was never meant to be run alone. It is through the support of others that we can cast off anything that hinders us. In what sometimes feels like an increasingly individualistic society, recognising that we run the race better if we run it with others is countercultural. But the beauty of the gospel and the Christian faith to which we hold is interconnected-ness – first expressed through the incarnation where God reaches out to humanity, and second through the importance of community, loving our neighbours as ourselves.

God, thank you that we do not run the race alone – but with you and with each other. May we show support to others in the races they are running today and always. Amen

CHINE MCDONALD

A new mind-pattern

Do not conform to the pattern of this world, but be transformed by the renewing of your mind. Then you will be able to test and approve what God's will is – his good, pleasing and perfect will. (NIV)

The ways of the kingdom of God are profoundly different to those of the world. When God finished his creation, he called it 'good'; but envy, hatred and sin have since entered the world, and things are not as he intended them to be.

When I read the news, the headlines are filled with stories of things that are displeasing to God: nation rising against nation in conflict and strife; people turning to violence, killing and brutalising each other; bodies sold into slavery, to serve the selfish desires of others; the world burning because we have not been good stewards of the earth as God commanded.

God's kingdom is one of hope and life. To see that goodness and light in a world full of darkness and despair is an act of hopeful defiance. We can choose not to conform to the pattern of this world; to choose love where there is hate, choose servanthood instead of seeking dominion; to see every person – no matter their background, race or gender – as someone made in the image of God and worthy of innate dignity, value and worth.

It is so easy for our minds to conform to the world's way of thinking. But today's passage is a reminder to us of the instruction that we, as followers of Christ, are not to think as the world thinks. It is possible for our minds to be changed, transformed and renewed. How wonderful to have the promise of what comes after the renewal of our minds – the ability to test and approve what God's will is. While the world's ways can be destructive and dark, God's will is good, pleasing and perfect.

Lord of all, thank you that your Holy Spirit can renew and transform our minds. Help us to see things as you see them. In Jesus' name. Amen

CHINE MCDONALD

Put your hands to good work

Anyone who has been stealing must steal no longer, but must work, doing something useful with their own hands, that they may have something to share with those in need. (NIV)

There may be a temptation when reading today's passage to see ourselves as holy people. I know I did, initially. When we read about stealing and theft, we might think we can skip over those admonitions because we are not burglars or crooks, nor do we make our living out of conning people. These things obviously run counter to following Jesus.

But throughout the New Testament there are warnings about people who see themselves as pious and holy. Instead, we should ask ourselves what these verses could be saying to us. Whether or not we have taken physical things that do not belong to us – money, jewellery, staplers from work or other material items – the sin in each of us makes it possible for us to rob others of their joy or their sense of dignity.

I love that Paul goes on to describe an alternative vision, which is rooted in this idea that we can all be part of each other's flourishing. What we do with our bodies can help to shape a better world. By doing 'something useful' with our hands, we create something that enables us to change the world.

I love the example of Sarah Corbett, a Christian who founded the Craftivist Collective – a group of people committed to using thoughtful, beautiful crafts to encourage themselves and others to make a positive change in the world. So many of us have got out of touch with using our hands to create beauty. I've found that having a toddler has unleashed a long-buried creativity, a desire to use the everyday things we find – in nature or things that would otherwise be put in the rubbish bin – to create something wonderful.

Creator God, who makes dry bones live, help us to breathe life into desolate places. Help us to create beautiful things that help change our world. In Jesus' name, we pray. Amen

CHINE MCDONALD

The body: unified yet distinct

For just as each of us has one body with many members, and these members do not all have the same function, so in Christ we, though many, form one body, and each member belongs to all the others.
(NIV)

I was one of those children who loved team sports at school. From the first time I played netball at the age of nine, I fell in love with it. It was my absolute favourite and I continued to play in secondary school and university, and even played for one or two office teams as an adult.

Part of the reason why I loved netball was the clarity there was in people's roles. I only ever played one position: Goal Shooter. I was tall, did not like running and liked the thrill of scoring the points. In netball, each player has a defined role – to defend, to attack, to score, to see the opportunities for the team and play a central role. In the game, each member is an individual. No one has the same function as anyone else. When the game is played at its best, you see the beauty in the unified yet distinct parts coming together for a purpose.

Today's passage reminds us of the way in which each member of the body of Christ has a unique role to play, too. Every member of the body is fearfully and wonderfully made, and uniquely and highly valued by God. When each of us is both valued and living with a purpose that we know God has marked out for us, while also knowing that we are loved by a supportive community of believers, we will feel secure in who we are and ready to do what God has called us to do, to run the race marked out for us. Though we are many, we form one body, and belong to each other.

Father God, thank you that each of us is unique in your eyes and we can trust in your plans for our lives. May we be people of purpose and build up other members of the family. In Jesus' name. Amen

CHINE MCDONALD

The words of our mouths

Do not let any unwholesome talk come out of your mouths, but only what is helpful for building others up according to their needs, that it may benefit those who listen. (NIV)

Since having a child, I have become much more aware of the words that come out of my mouth. I am conscious that my husband and I are responsible for shaping a young life that we hope will grow into a kind, loving, intelligent, curious, adventurous and secure man of God.

When we look back, we might realise that the words our parents or guardians spoke to us when we were young children have influenced who we have become and the way that we have thought about ourselves and others. Words are capable of building people up, and they have the ability to tear people down.

I want my son to hear only words from my mouth that are helpful in building him up. It feels so easy to do that when thinking about my child, but I also realise how often I fail in the words I speak about or in front of other people.

When I was at school, I went through a period of taking a swear jar around with me and elicited donations for charities every time someone swore in my presence. Looking back, I must have come across as a holier-than-thou religious sort who wanted to ruin people's fun. But we know that when the Bible mentions unwholesome talk, it is not just aimed at the potty-mouthed among us. Unwholesome talk includes speaking badly about each other, gossiping or repeating negative thoughts about ourselves and about our friends, family, neighbours and colleagues.

So I am challenged today to watch what I'm saying, to speak hope and life wherever I am, for in that way I can reflect the goodness of God and the Holy Spirit at work in me, who enables me to be far better than I am in my own flesh.

Father, we are sorry for the times we have let unwholesome talk come out of our mouths. Help us to keep watch over our words; may our mouths speak in a way that builds others up, for the sake of your kingdom. Amen

CHINE MCDONALD

Our bodies are temples

Flee from sexual immorality. All other sins a person commits are outside the body, but whoever sins sexually, sins against their own body. Do you not know that your bodies are temples of the Holy Spirit…? You were bought at a price. Therefore, honour God with your bodies. (NIV)

I wanted to skip over today's passage. I have attempted to avoid it, to skate over these difficult words and pretend that they are not there. The themes spoken about here in 1 Corinthians are not ones that might be included in polite conversation. They cover topics such as sex, slavery, prostitution and the gratification of the flesh.

Like many teenagers growing up in the church who had committed their lives to Jesus, sex was something I thought often about. It was as if to abstain from sex was the thing that made us truly Christian – the defining mark between true salvation and hell.

As I've grown older and sex has become more than the obsession of a hormonal teenager, I have come to terms with why passages such as this exist. The Bible tells us that our bodies are temples of the Holy Spirit, that we belong to God and were bought at a price. I have been so disappointed to hear stories of well-known Christian leaders who preach purity, yet whose sex lives have fallen far short of what God would hope for us.

But it is not necessarily the physical acts that make sexual immorality so against God's plan, but the way in which people who commit these acts of immorality treat other people who are also made in God's image. Not only are we temples of the Holy Spirit, but also every human being is more than just a body to be used for fleeting sexual pleasure. There is a lesson in this for each and every one of us. Loving one another as God has loved us requires honouring others' bodies just as we honour God with ours.

God who nourishes our souls with good things, give us strength to flee from anything that does not honour you. May we see each person as someone worthy of dignity and made in your divine image. In Jesus' name. Amen

CHINE MCDONALD

A cheerful heart

A cheerful heart is good medicine, but a crushed spirit dries up the bones. (NIV)

A friend of mine spoke recently about a childhood memory. Every day without fail, when he returned home from school, his mum used to turn on the music and make him dance before he had said a word. Her premise was that no matter how bad things had been that day, however difficult the situations he had faced, by moving his body in time to the music he would feel a sense of happiness. Whatever might have been weighing him down would be made a little less unbearable.

Since hearing this, I have tried it a few times with my son. But as I bop up and down to the music, he looks at me with the disdain that only a two-year-old can muster and asks: 'What *are* you doing?' Maybe I will leave it a few more years to implement this particular tradition. But regardless of whether he has joined me, I have felt the cares and worries of the day melt away as I dance to the music.

Proverbs 17 lists several ways in which people's inward attitudes, hearts and behaviours affect their physical bodies and vice versa. Having a heart that is cheerful, happy or joyful can affect our physical well-being. I'm sure you have felt the interaction between how you are feeling on the inside and how that manifests itself on the outside. When my soul is singing, people often tell me I look well, but when I'm feeling down or depressed, it is impossible to hide this in my outer demeanour. It is wonderful to realise just how much God cares about us as whole people – inside and out.

Creator God, help us to be bringers of joy, speaking hope and life into every situation. Amen

CHINE MCDONALD

Seeing as God sees

'For the Lord sees not as man sees: man looks on the outward appearance, but the Lord looks on the heart.' (ESV)

Our world is obsessed with image. People in the public eye – especially women – are often judged on what they look like and how they dress, more than on the content of their character.

In my first book, *Am I Beautiful?*, I explored the ways in which all women, including Christian women, are negatively impacted by the pressure society places on us to look a certain way. There is an arbitrary standard of beauty that is held up as the ideal and every woman is judged on this standard, even though God loves each of us equally regardless of how we look. Every one of us is fearfully and wonderfully made and possesses the *imago Dei* (image of God). Since we are made in the image of God and have something of the essence of God in each of us, we are worthy of innate dignity, value and worth.

When I think about the way in which women are judged on their appearance, and particularly those moments when I feel un-beautiful because of this standard, I remember today's verse. Although God made our whole beings – our souls, our minds and our bodies – he does not look at the outward appearance as humans are prone to doing.

In the story of David's anointing from which today's verse comes, we see how God chooses surprising people to use for his purposes. Though the obvious candidate for king might have been Eliab – the one who looked the part – God paid no regard to his appearance or his height, but chose the unexpected. How wonderful to worship a God who sees the beauty inside each of us.

Loving God, help us to see each other through your eyes; people made in your image, wholly loved and precious. Amen

                                                          CHINE MCDONALD

Outwardly ageing, inwardly serving

Therefore we do not lose heart. Though outwardly we are wasting away, yet inwardly we are being renewed day by day. (NIV)

Ingrid Bergman once said: 'Getting old is like climbing a mountain; you get a little out of breath, but the view is much better.' These words are comforting in a world that can often make us afraid of ageing.

I have noticed that the older I get, the longer things seem to take: getting up from a seat, going on a run, chasing after my toddler. I watch my son and marvel at the ease with which he jumps up and down, runs around in circles, bends over and touches his toes. No creaks or groans like those of his parents! It feels sometimes like our bodies are 'wasting away', and the energy of our younger days seems very distant.

People have long been in search of the elixir of youth, hidden their grey hairs and lied about their age, making themselves appear younger than they are. In certain societies, including where I am from in Nigeria, elders are revered and respected, their wisdom seen as vital for the benefit of the whole community. Where there is a positive view of ageing, those who are getting older are less likely to 'lose heart' because of the value placed upon their years.

In God's kingdom, each of us is of value – no matter our age. Today's passage is again a reminder that God looks at what is inside – our hearts and relationship with him – rather than the external, which he sees as less important. No matter how long we have on this earth, we are encouraged to use our bodies – our tired, creaky, ageing bodies that are wasting away – to honour God.

God who gives us strength, help us not to lose heart, though we feel fatigued and tired. Lord, would you renew our strength so that we can soar like eagles and live lives worthy of your name. Amen

CHINE MCDONALD

Taking care of our bodies

No one ever hated their own body, but they feed and care for their body, just as Christ does the church – for we are members of his body. (NIV)

I am looking forward to a spa weekend in a few days' time with two female friends. I cannot wait to relax and unwind, to release the tension that has been building up in my body for months.

Our bodies take on so much of the stress and strain of our daily lives. Whether it is through our work lives hunched over laptops, with our eyes becoming blurry from looking at screens all day, or our feet pounding the streets as we try to beat our personal bests, or the strain of picking up and running after children– our bodies are often so tired that we do not have time to stop and hear what they need.

My friends and I booked our spa weekend because we recognised that feeding and caring for our bodies was much needed after months – or even years – of keeping going and putting our bodies under immense strain.

There are some people who believe that Christianity teaches that the body is bad, and that we should almost overcome it to be true believers. But, while there are warnings throughout the Bible telling us to stay away from things that harm our bodies and subsequently ourselves – gluttony and drunkenness, for example – today's passage shows that our bodies in themselves are good, reflecting God's good creation. Taking care of our bodies is a way to show that we value ourselves.

These verses show us how caring for our bodies reflects how Christ cares for the church. We are members of his body, so he does not want us to feel burdened or heavy-laden. He takes care of us, just as we should take care of our own bodies. In doing so, we show honour to God.

Lord, thank you that we have the privilege of being members of your body, through Christ's sacrifice on the cross. Amen

CHINE MCDONALD

From the inside out

Rather, clothe yourselves with the Lord Jesus Christ, and do not think about how to gratify the desires of the flesh. (NIV)

I have recently lost a significant amount of weight. The pounds had been slowly but surely creeping on as the busyness of life meant I was paying less attention to the food I was consuming. I had lost all sense of balance, with butter and oil used to turn even the most nutritious of vegetables into calorie-laden feasts.

I knew I was not happy with my weight, but hoped that no one had noticed. Until someone made a comment that made me feel mortified, embarrassed and ashamed. But it was the kick-start I needed to make a life change. And so it was that I took myself off to a local slimming club and stepped on the scales to begin a journey of readjusting my relationship with food.

One of the key things I have learnt over the past few months is that it is never really about the food itself. There are deeply held beliefs we hold about ourselves that fuel these unhealthy habits. Those of us who struggle with weight issues often do not see our bodies as worthy of care. Perhaps we are feeding an inner sense of dissatisfaction by attempting to gratify the desires of the flesh.

The behaviour shift in my eating habits has been intentional. One of the primary guidelines is about being planned and focused, and I have found it revolutionary. The things I used to eat – the stodgy and unhealthy foods, the sweet treats – have become almost invisible to me now.

I love the intentionality of the instruction given in today's passage: clothe yourselves with the Lord Jesus Christ. This is all we need to do to change ourselves – from the inside out.

Lord, we are sorry for the times we have sought to gratify the desires of the flesh. Help us to fix our eyes on you. Amen

CHINE MCDONALD

But the flesh is weak

Then he returned to his disciples and found them sleeping. 'Couldn't you men keep watch with me for one hour?' he asked Peter. 'Watch and pray so that you will not fall into temptation. The spirit is willing, but the flesh is weak.' (NIV)

When it comes to spiritual matters and my relationship with God, I confess that sometimes my spirit is willing, but my flesh is weak. I find this most true of my prayer life. I can imagine how the disciples must have felt when Jesus rebuked them for failing to keep watch with him: disappointed, ashamed and embarrassed. They probably felt they had let Jesus down. I can hear the exasperation in Jesus' voice – it sounds like this might have been a common occurrence and that the disciples had done this before.

When I dedicate time to prayer, it seems like there is always something more urgent and important than spending time in quiet contemplation. The devil, who roams around waiting to destroy, does not want us to spend time watching and praying. He knows that it is dangerous, that what the people of God can do if they humble themselves, using their bodies in prayer, could be catastrophic for his kingdom.

Like many Christians, I have learned that the discipline of 'keeping watch', spending time with Jesus and inviting the Holy Spirit in, puts things into perspective. Cultivating our relationship with God helps us to see the world differently. We recognise that our lives should be refocused on knowing God and seeing how we can love, support and encourage others towards having a relationship with God, too.

What is inevitable, though, is that at times we will slip up. Like the disciples, Christ will find us having fallen asleep. But let us be encouraged that these sleepy disciples ended up being the ones who turned the world upside down when they discovered the good news of Christ's death and resurrection.

Lord, we are sorry for the times our flesh has been weak. Help us to keep watch, praying for your mighty kingdom to come on earth as it is in heaven. Amen
CHINE MCDONALD

Opening our arms

She sees that her trading is profitable, and her lamp does not go out at night. In her hand she holds the distaff and grasps the spindle with her fingers. She opens her arms to the poor and extends her hands to the needy. (NIV)

Today's reading is taken from one of the most famous passages in the Bible, especially when it comes to women's ministry. This description of a wife of noble character has often been presented as an example of the perfect woman.

Many of us fall into the trap of doing too much in that quest to be shining examples of womanhood. I admit that one of my favourite compliments is when someone tells me they think I am superwoman. I seem to get a thrill out of thinking I have successfully managed to spin all the plates and juggle all the balls without anyone seeing any of them dropping. It is, however, exhausting.

So often our lives can be full of taking care of friends and family, work and other pursuits in the quest to achieve. Sometimes, when I look at the description of the Proverbs 31 woman, I wonder when she has a moment to herself, to feed her own mind, body and soul. When I read that her lamp does not go out at night, I am reminded of those times many of us burn the candle at both ends, never stopping to pause or take a breath.

This woman uses her body to glorify God through her work and her care for others, including extending her hands to those in need. For some of us, that means working in caring professions, taking care of those with physical or emotional needs – the homeless, the elderly, those who have physical disabilities or those in poverty. For others, it might mean taking care of the ones around us who need us. Whatever God calls us to do as women today, may we do it to bring glory and honour to his name.

Pause and reflect on what God has called you uniquely to do today. Take a look at your diary to find the space to be still in his presence.

CHINE MCDONALD

A study of Micah

Sara Batts-Neale writes:

Micah is one of the twelve minor prophets. It is one of the books I always need to use the contents page to look up! In the next two weeks we will journey through condemnation, lament and hope – taking in history, social justice and ethics. As we read, we will seek to understand that little bit more of Israel's history and the contemporary situation into which Micah was speaking.

The reigns of kings Jotham, Ahaz and Hezekiah of Judah end somewhere around 727BC. The story of Hezekiah's reign is told in 2 Kings 18—20. At that time, the land in which the tribes of Israel settled had split into the northern and southern kingdoms of Judah and Israel (represented in Micah's prophecies by their capitals, Jerusalem and Samaria). The Assyrians were the most powerful people in the region, and their expansion threatened all countries. By 727BC Israel and Judah were reduced to vassal states. Hezekiah was king, but king of a state controlled by the Assyrians, who demanded taxing tribute.

After the conquering Assyrian ruler died, Israel rebelled. That led to a counterattack in which Samaria was destroyed after a siege lasting three years. Micah 1:2–7 draws on this event: Samaria, says the prophet, has been destroyed by God.

I think it is important to understand this geopolitical situation. It helps us make sense of the oracles and the way in which prophets related threats to security from the activity of external forces to the behaviour of God's chosen people. Isaiah was a contemporary of Micah.

In his warnings of disaster, Micah also sets out what a righteous life looks like. He calls out injustice. He champions the downtrodden and castigates the powerful. The command to do justice, love mercy and walk humbly with our God is a simple and clear principle.

I find it sobering how our contemporary structures mirror the inherent unfairness Micah describes. He was an outsider, and that gives us food for thought, too. To whose voice do we listen? Would a prophet like Micah be heard over the clamour of the rich and powerful today? Whose opinions matter to us?

Understanding the oracle

The word of the Lord that came to Micah of Moresheth in the days of Kings Jotham, Ahaz, and Hezekiah of Judah, which he saw concerning Samaria and Jerusalem. (NRSV)

This opening verse establishes Micah as a prophet and explains the context in which he was preaching. Micah's name means 'Who is like God?', which clearly tells us there is, in fact, none like God.

Today's reading is a general oracle; in later days we will read of the specifics of Judah's transgressions and sins. Fundamentally, transgression means not keeping the covenant. God's chosen people were in a covenant relationship with him. God led them to freedom, gave them land and asked them to do what is right. As a basis, the ten commandments given in Exodus 20 set out the way of righteousness. Yet, as we shall see, the covenant had been well and truly forgotten.

Verse 7 begins to show the problem. 'All her idols I will lay waste.' I don't think it is a coincidence that the first accusation reflects the first commandment. Idols make no demands on their worshippers. Idols are passive. Whatever rituals are created around them are made by people for people, not by God for his people or by people in order to worship their creator. Idols were a tangible symbol of a people who had forgotten who their true God was.

It is very easy to hold things that are not God in the same regard as God. If love of God and seeking to do his will are not the things that guide us in life, something else will take their place at the heart of our being. The imagery in this passage reminds us of the power of our God. We should not underestimate his majesty and his awesomeness. He deserves first place in our life.

Lord, thank you for the people, places and things that help me focus on you. Help me to understand where I do not put you first in life. Amen

SARA BATTS-NEALE

Oracles of doom

For this I will lament and wail; I will go barefoot and naked. (NRSV)

Is the British stiff upper lip a thing of the past? Keeping calm and carrying on isn't always the best option in the face of major tragedy or collective loss. I think these days we funnel our angst into protest and demonstration, the closest thing we have to a communal lament that enables people to let out a wail of pain and loss.

Today we hear the voice of Micah, lamenting the fate of his people in the face of international political crisis, interpreted as direct punishment from God. Lament has a sense of regret, as well as sorrow. Micah knows what will lie ahead; he sees the destruction that is coming and that it cannot be stopped.

There is plenty of that lament in the Bible, particularly in the psalms, so Micah is in keeping with ancient tradition. There is also clever wordplay too, which we often miss because we're reading the English translation of the Hebrew.

In today's verses, we could be tempted to skip over place names we find hard to read. Without knowing their meanings, we miss the wordplay that helps shape the oracle. Shaphir, whose inhabitants will be naked and shamed, means 'beauty town'. Beth-leaphrah means 'house of dust'. Rolling in dust was an established way of expressing the grief that comes from a humiliation. Zaanan – whose inhabitants do not go forth – means 'going forth town'.

Finally, 'the glory of Israel shall come to Adullam' (v. 15). Adullam is a place to flee: it's where David went to hide from Saul (1 Samuel 22:1). These name-appropriate statements help to emphasise the coming doom and remind us that their downfall will be comprehensive.

Have you ever seen a problem looming and not felt listened to? Is there a situation now you are aware of that you can bring to God?

SARA BATTS-NEALE

Getting away with daylight robbery

They covet fields, and seize them; houses, and take them away; they oppress householder and house, people and their inheritance. (NRSV)

Chapter 2 begins to explain exactly what the people have done that has broken the covenant with God. The powerful are abusing their authority. They do what is wrong in plain sight – when the morning dawns – because they know that with a corrupt justice system they can, literally, get away with daylight robbery.

At the time Micah was writing, owning land wasn't only an insurance policy against old age or an inheritance for the next generation, but also freedom, security and provision for the here and now. Micah accuses the powerful of depriving people of their rightful possession on a whim. Those made landless and homeless were driven into poverty.

So we see systematic exploitation and corruption of the covenant being laid bare. The command to not covet one's neighbour's possessions has been ignored. We begin to understand that Micah is shining a light on abuses that have been perpetrated by those at the top of the system. He points not to individuals but to a whole society.

I am struck by how little has changed in many parts of the world. The misuse of power at the expense of the powerless is a constant theme. Land and water have become assets to be grabbed – and with crime in some places almost consequence-free, violence is the norm. Major corporations buy land as an investment, forcing farmers off land they have tended for generations.

In many places, the powerful operate with impunity. We regularly read of exploitation of the weak by the strong – whether that's drug gangs preying on the misfit youngster, the inhumanity of modern slavery or scammers exploiting the fears of the elderly. People lose security and their future is blighted. Injustices documented thousands of years ago are still seen today.

Lord, help me open my eyes to the injustices around me. Give strength to those who help the marginalised find their voice to speak out, and help me listen to their stories with compassion. Amen

SARA BATTS-NEALE

Preaching to the indifferent

If someone were to go about uttering empty falsehoods, saying, 'I will preach to you of wine and strong drink,' such a one would be the preacher for this people! (NRSV)

Preaching is a joy, and a major responsibility. I have the joy of helping others understand the word of God, and I have the responsibility to ensure I'm not just telling people what they want to hear. When I finished my curacy last year, one farewell email said how much my sermons would be missed, 'even if some had ruffled feathers at times'.

I don't think the sender realised how much I would take that as a compliment. Early on in ministry, I remember second-guessing myself a lot and worrying about what I was going to say – then realising that I would not be fulfilling my vocation if I only preached words which left a congregation comfortable and complacent.

However, no one has actually told me to stop preaching yet, unlike today's passage, in which the powerful try to silence Micah. They are absolutely sure that there will be no comeback for their behaviour; they are, after all, used to acting with impunity.

Micah's intervention and his prophetic highlighting of injustice are merely irritations to be ignored. The powerful think that he can be silenced. They sound here an awful lot like they're just putting their fingers in their ears and singing, 'La la la, can't hear you!' They're not interested in preaching that will challenge them or that will show them the way back to the life the covenant with God demands.

What they really want is someone who will preach of uncomplicated, pleasurable things – someone who will gloss over the homelessness they cause; their indifference towards the suffering that is caused to children; the loss of dignity caused by the seizing of a robe. Micah's warnings are not for them.

Lord, open the eyes and ears of those who need to hear your word. I pray for those who preach unwelcome messages, that you will give them courage to speak out to those who would ignore you. Amen

SARA BATTS-NEALE

Restoration and reassurance

I will set them together like sheep in a fold, like a flock in its pasture; it will resound with people. (NRSV)

I have recently been reading about sheep farming in the Lake District and Wales and learning about sheep being 'hefted' to their place. Sheep know their grazing places; and they don't stray too far into neighbouring farms' allocated bits of hillside. Ewes somehow teach it to their lambs, so the next generation know where they belong, too. I found this such a powerful image of security, and it came to me again when I read verse 12 of today's short reading.

We switch to the voice of the Lord God, issuing a promise to those who will be left behind. The Lord promises the people will be safe, like a flock in its pasture, like a sheep in a fold. The Bible is full of references to the safety of sheep under the hands of an experienced shepherd – Psalm 23 makes this explicit and is such a well-loved idea for many. These notions of hope and care stand in contrast to the oracle of doom that we have so far encountered in Micah.

It's thought this passage could refer specifically to the release from the siege of Jerusalem by the Assyrian ruler Sennacherib, recounted in 2 Kings 18. Jerusalem was the only city not taken by Sennacherib in his campaign against cities in Judah. 2 Kings 19:35 ascribes the defeat to an angel of the Lord striking down 185,000 Assyrians, forcing a retreat by Sennacherib.

The imagery is thus very vivid – the leader breaking out of the fortified gates at the end of the siege, the peace and security of its people. It is a message of hope delivered in bleak times, of the restoration of rightful order with the king and the Lord at the head of the crowd.

Where do you feel safe? Let us give thanks to God today for times and places of security, and pray for those living in stressful and dangerous situations.

SARA BATTS-NEALE

Exploitation exposed

Should you not know justice? – you who hate the good and love the evil. (NRSV)

On Tuesday we read how Micah laid out charges against the powerful and the corrupt in society. Today the imagery intensifies as chapter 3 opens with an oracle of judgement. There is a command to listen, an accusation and a sentence to be passed.

I don't think Micah was really accusing the judges of actual cannibalism. But I find it a commanding metaphor. Paying poverty wages that lead to health inequalities and reduced life expectancy – is that not also fatal exploitation?

As I write, we are facing the economic consequences of what will probably be known as the first wave of Covid-19 lockdowns, and then we have the end of the Brexit transition period. I am anxious about how things will be when these notes come to be read. I am anxious about how well those in power listen to the charities and campaign groups who highlight the hardships many live with. Prophecy is a critique of current situations as much as warnings about things to come. Prophets try to open people's eyes to the present reality and how the future could be different.

False prophets lead people further astray from the kind of righteous living that the Lord requires. Instead of standing up for those on the margins of society, they declare war on those with nothing. This is another example of the exploitation of the weakest that runs throughout the book of Micah.

In contrast, Micah reminds us that he is full of the Spirit of the Lord, full of power and justice. He alone has authority to show where the people have been in breach of the covenant – where they have sinned. Only Micah has the power to tell it like it is.

God of our understanding, in a world of competing voices, help us listen and help us to find the truth. Amen

SARA BATTS-NEALE

Ethical dilemmas

Its rulers give judgement for a bribe, its priests teach for a price, its prophets give oracles for money; yet they lean upon the Lord and say, 'Surely the Lord is with us! No harm shall come upon us.' (NRSV)

The second oracle in chapter 3 takes us further into the iniquities of the leaders. We have seen already what injustices and false prophecies are like. Now we see that the priests themselves have a price. One of the key themes in Micah's prophecy is the lack of justice and equity, and this is spelled out here very plainly.

But the most important thing in today's reading is the idea that the leaders were working with a half-truth. They leant on the Lord, they continued their rituals and claimed that God was on their side. But what they chose to forget was that God's presence depended on the ethical behaviour of those who kept the covenant.

I believe we are also called to an ethical life. It is no good us attending church on a Sunday if our behaviour on a Monday is no different from anyone else. We are Christians 24 hours a day, seven days a week. Do the choices we make reflect our obedience to God, to Jesus' command to love one another, our reliance on the steering hand of the Holy Spirit?

Ethics is often presented as a moral dilemma – a choice between two outcomes, both with difficult consequences. A rounded life is based on what is called virtue ethics. The idea of 'virtue' has lost some of its helpfulness lately. 'Virtue signalling' – posting on social media about a choice or a campaign to paint oneself in a positive light – has undermined the idea. Faith, hope and love – these are the theological virtues we can practise living out in our daily lives. Faith in the God we know is present. Hope for the future outworking of the kingdom. Love for our neighbour and ourselves.

Loving God, when I am not sure what to do or say, guide me in the ways of faith, hope and love. Help me to make good choices so that I may be seen as your child in the world. Amen

SARA BATTS-NEALE

Climb every mountain...

'Come, let us go up to the mountain of the Lord, to the house of the God of Jacob; that he may teach us his ways and that we may walk in his paths.' (NRSV)

The end of chapter 3 foresaw a time when all signs of worship had been removed. Here, we have a shift of mood into one of confidence, and a shift of narrative from devastation to restoration. In a reversal of fortune, all nations will be drawn to Jerusalem and the God of Jacob.

Some years ago, I briefly visited the Austrian Tyrol. I spent a day walking around a lake at Pertisau, the backdrop to a favourite set of stories. However, I had to imagine the glorious mountains because of low cloud and drizzle. It didn't matter, because it was enough just to soak up the atmosphere (literally!). Tall peaks, pointing heavenward – so much a symbol of our ascent into God's presence. Vast, immovable features. No wonder in chapter 1 God's power was represented by his ability to flatten them!

The path to the top of the mountain is often difficult, full of trials and setbacks. It's a well-used metaphor for the Christian life. We speak of mountaintop experiences – the exhilarating sense of being in God's presence, of being infilled with the Spirit – when everything makes sense and we can see our path and the landscape laid out ahead of us.

If only the path we took down from the mountain was straightforward. But, more often than not, the paths we take in life provide us with ample opportunity to practise our virtue, to lean on God and to admit the mistakes we've made. The important thing is to keep walking – whether that's a tentative shuffle or a leap like a mountain goat! Some days are easier than others, some mistakes easier to correct, some situations easier to navigate. But we can travel secure in the knowledge that we walk in the paths of the Lord.

What does life hold for you today? Glorious views, where everything seems clear, or a struggle to find any path that leads in the right direction? Reach out to God in thanks or for help and he will listen.

SARA BATTS-NEALE

The price of hope

There you shall be rescued, there the Lord will redeem you from the hands of your enemies. (NRSV)

Yesterday we read of the hope of Judah. Today we learn the price that must be paid for that restoration: exile.

The book of Micah was not written at one time and at one sitting. There's a strongly supported idea that bits of it were written much later than King Hezekiah's reign, perhaps during or after the Babylonian exile (586–538BC). Remember that the overrunning of Israel and Judah by foreign forces was interpreted as God's method of disciplining the people who had ignored their covenant relationship with him. The land God gave was contingent on their following the law and commandments; they had become corrupt, so the land was then taken away. Restoration in 537BC under the reign of Cyrus was, therefore, the return of God's favour.

There is a simple danger that if we use this kind of punishment-restoration reasoning too glibly, we can view misfortunes as punishment from God, or blame ourselves for not being good enough. That hurts us, and others. Just as we experience the joy of the mountain, where we feel close to God and sure of our faith, we all have times when we are in the open plain – times when we feel cut off from all that is familiar and sustains us. Faith falters; our purpose in life is called into question.

Sometimes this happens after a major loss or change; other times we drift into the wilderness without noticing. Others suffer the pain of rejection by family or church. These times can be profoundly painful, and not all of us will find the longed-for restoration and resolution. We have hope, though, that the things that are incomprehensible to us make sense to the Lord, whose thoughts we do not know.

Heavenly Father, when I feel lost, show me your way. When I feel lonely and abandoned, show me my companions. Thank you for your promises of healing and hope. Amen

SARA BATTS-NEALE

A brief diversion to Advent

But you, O Bethlehem of Ephrathah, who are one of the little clans of Judah, from you shall come forth for me one who is to rule in Israel, whose origin is from of old, from ancient days. (NRSV)

Today's extract may be a familiar one. In churches that follow the lectionary, it's an Advent reading every third year; it's paraphrased in Matthew 2:6 when we read of the visit of the wise men. This is a passage that is established as a Messianic prophecy – a clear foreshadowing of the coming of Jesus. So we switch from Micah's highlighting what is wrong in the present to predicting that which is to come.

We know about Bethlehem: the little town, royal David's city. The link between David and the new ruler to come is made clear – we are going right back to the place where David's line began, to the lowly, inauspicious place, with the birth of the Messiah to take place in a lowly, insignificant space.

As Jesus himself teaches us in Matthew 20, the last will be first and the first will be last. These are the topsy-turvy values of God's kingdom. The powerful will lose their power. What's left – the remnant – will be preserved and restored to glory. As the pregnant Mary's glorious song in Luke 1:46–55 tells us, the rich will be sent away empty; the proud scattered; the hungry filled with good things.

What else will this ruler do? We return to the shepherd. David, Israel's ideal ruler, was the shepherd boy, so images of shepherding also remind Micah's hearers what it was like to be led by someone who walked closely with God. So this passage points to the coming of Christ and establishes him as one who is from David. That means his credentials as a leader are not in doubt. We need to know that Jesus, born ignominiously in the stable, is going to be a great bringer of peace and security.

Heavenly Father, we thank you for sending us your Son. We thank you for the scriptures we have that unfold your story of salvation. Amen

SARA BATTS-NEALE

Which side are you on?

Then the remnant of Jacob, surrounded by many peoples, shall be like dew from the Lord, like showers on the grass, which do not depend upon people or wait for any mortal. (NRSV)

The remainder of chapter 5 brings two different messages – there is salvation for some, but destruction for others.

The remnant of Jacob will be blessed. Water – in the form of dew and showers – is a sign of blessing for those who will be left. They will become strong, free from adversaries and enemies. We again have a sense of security and peacefulness being restored. But for those who continue to reject God, the future is clear.

Verses 10–15 aren't just a random list of punishments to be meted out; they reflect three very specific ways in which people have rejected God. They have, instead, put their trust in military power, in sorcery and in idols, and these will be systematically removed.

We have been reading doom-laden prophecies and threats of devastation for several days now. I wonder if this kind of promised destruction has made us question our image of God. Many people throughout the ages have struggled with the portrayal of God as vengeful and demanding. Some, like Marcion in the first century, strove to remove all traces of the God of the Old Testament entirely. He took all the references to Hebrew scriptures out of the writings he had.

We need to be wary we don't fall into the same trap and ignore what we learn about God's activity before Jesus' birth. There is no doubt that it is challenging to read that the God we love and worship will destroy towns in anger and wrath. The broader story of God's revelation, his patience and his love can be obscured by the violence. It is an unpredictable and complicated view of God – but it is the same God we know of through Jesus in the New Testament.

God of history, we thank you for the unfolding story of your works of salvation. Help us to wrestle with your word. Give us teachers to help us understand and know your ways more clearly. Amen

SARA BATTS-NEALE

Guidance for life

He has told you, O mortal, what is good; and what does the Lord require of you but to do justice, and to love kindness, and to walk humbly with your God? (NRSV)

Micah 6:8 is for me the beating heart of the whole prophecy. Actually, I was tempted to write all this whole fortnight's reflections on these verses alone…

First, though, let's look at verse 4. Miriam gets a mention! I want us to be excited by that. Miriam was a prophet too – Exodus 15:20 tells us this.

We know how often the women in the Bible are ignored. So I want us to celebrate the female prophet – and in that celebration to remind ourselves that our voices can be heard. We can speak up for what we know to be right. Yours may well be the prophetic voice your community needs to hear to help it do what is good.

And what is good? Justice, kindness and aligning ourselves with God's will. Walking humbly with God doesn't mean berating ourselves as worthless. That is a misunderstanding of humility. It means taming our pride – our belief that we can do life better by ourselves – and it means trusting in God. It also means true repentance – true examination of the ways in which we've fallen short and honestly bringing those difficulties to God. Micah's people heaped sacrifice on sacrifice to no avail because these were just empty rituals. They would make a sacrifice to say sorry and then continue on their way of exploitation and oppression.

Justice is broader than the legal concepts of guilt and innocence. It is the idea that each individual matters, that society is fair and equal and that rights are recognised. The opposite, in fact, of the society Micah describes where property is confiscated on a whim by the powerful and a corrupt leadership works in its own self-interest.

Kindness – well, that should be straightforward. But we do need to remember to be kind to ourselves, too!

Where can you speak up? Does the idea of your voice being heard excite you, or is it a scary prospect? Let us give thanks to God for Miriam and the women she has inspired, who in turn inspire us.

SARA BATTS-NEALE

From lament to confidence

But as for me, I will look to the Lord, I will wait for the God of my salvation; my God will hear me. (NRSV)

We return to lament at the start of this chapter – 'Woe is me!' is the clue to this. Micah laments over the state of the country. There is nothing good left: no fruit or grapes to satisfy hunger or thirst. There are no fruitful, faithful people to maintain the ethical aspects of the covenant life. All that are left are the corrupt officials, seeking their own self-interest. The social order is in disarray around him; no one can be trusted. The disintegration is seen in verse 6 as family loyalties break down. This state of chaotic change is quoted in Matthew 10:34–35 as Jesus warns of the persecution and trouble ahead for the disciples.

Micah's lament speaks of helplessness in the face of coming judgement. Yet it also speaks clearly of confidence in the salvation that will come and of the need to simply wait on the Lord.

In times of vulnerability, perhaps the only option – and thus the most powerful option – is just to wait. In our own lives, waiting out a storm may be a better idea than raging against it. Difficult situations that we cannot change sap our energy if we rail against them. That's not to say we should accept danger or abuse. But we know the cliché that 'time is a great healer' is true: waiting patiently for grief or loss to fade might be the only thing we can do.

And goodness me, how hard that can be! Patience has never been my strong point. I have watched others' prayers for ease answered as I sit with my own discomfort and wondered why – and I confess to less confidence at times than Micah expresses here. Yet deep down, I always know it to be true that 'my God will hear me'.

Thank you, Lord, for patience and trust, even if they come in small doses. Help me to live with the things I find difficult. Show me when to fight, and when to wait. Amen

SARA BATTS-NEALE

Repentance and restoration

He will again have compassion upon us; he will tread our iniquities under foot. You will cast all our sins into the depths of the sea. (NRSV)

Today we conclude on notes of hope and restoration. We return to the image of shepherding, of safety and security, of protection and provision. This is all quite different from the storms of destruction – this is the calm of green pasture, of rest, of spiritual nourishment.

Repentance is key. Yesterday we read of Jerusalem finally understanding how sinfulness led to God's indignation (v. 9). Confession of faith, with true repentance, provided the one way forward for God's people. The response to compassion means a hymn of praise takes shape. Verse 18 reminds us of Micah's name, meaning 'Who is like God?' – there is no one! No other god compares in his willingness to pardon sin, to create a clean slate and to show continuing loyalty to those who live the covenant.

After all, what is the point of prophecy if heeding the warnings doesn't lead to forgiveness? Just like Judah and Israel, we can be sure that if we truly understand where we have gone wrong, God will remove our sins from us. Confession is part of the way in which we walk humbly with God – understanding the worst bits of ourselves and being honest with God about our thoughts, feelings and actions. It's not an easy thing to do.

We probably won't like it when people care enough to honestly tell us when we're in the wrong. Yet at the level of both our own behaviour and that of the society in which we live, we need those voices. We need the prophets to open our eyes to the unkind or unjust behaviour that we overlook. I pray that we will listen well when we meet those prophets.

Thank you, Lord, for today's prophets. Thank you for people who point to your work in the world and help us to walk humbly with you. Give us courage to speak up for love and justice. Amen

SARA BATTS-NEALE

Gideon: an unlikely hero

Rosemary Green writes:

The history of the Israelites for two centuries after Joshua's death is an erratic one. The people served the Lord throughout Joshua's lifetime and the elders who outlived him. They had experienced 'all the great things the Lord had done for Israel' (Judges 2:7, NIV) in the wilderness, crossing the Jordan and witnessing the destruction of Jericho. Then began a recurrent cycle. Failure to eradicate the pagan inhabitants of the land led to compromise with their Baal worship, directly disobeying the ten commandments: 'You shall have no other gods before me' and 'You shall not make for yourself an image in the form of anything in heaven above or on the earth beneath or in the waters below' (Exodus 20:3–4). God's anger was roused; they couldn't resist their enemies and he allowed their defeat, leading to servitude to the alien aggressors.

In their distress, they eventually cried out to a merciful God for relief – and he rescued them through divinely appointed judges, many of them unlikely saviours from a human viewpoint. Judges 2 sums it up; after each judge, a period of peace was followed by further disobedience, and the cycle continued.

One sad note of the book is a phrase we read twice (in 17:6 and 21:25). 'In those days Israel had no king; everyone did as they saw fit.' Anarchy and individualism reigned. It is not surprising they got in a mess. There are some clear lessons for us: the folly of ignoring God; the danger of intermarriage with those of other faiths and the ease of sliding into corrupt worship. And something we often overlook: God is angry with our unrighteousness – an anger that partners his love and mercy.

There is a useful framework for looking at a biblical character. 1) The background into which the person came. 2) The early years. 3) God's preparation. 4) Their relationship with God. 5) Their main work. 6) What happened later, good or bad. 7) Other Bible references. 8) Lessons for us to learn. While not following that framework rigorously, I have had it in mind in thinking about Gideon.

So, this next week we will follow the story of God's rescue of Israel through this young man, who thought himself small and unimportant. Our God can use insignificant people to do great things, if they listen and obey.

You did not listen

'I delivered you from the hand of all your oppressors… I said to you, "I am the Lord your God; do not worship the gods of the Amorites, in whose land you live." But you have not listened to me.' (NIV)

It was some 70 years since Joshua had led the people across the Jordan after their (unnecessary) 40 years of wandering in the wilderness. Before his death they had firmly committed themselves to serving the Lord (Joshua 24:21–24), but they soon forgot that promise. After 40 years of peace, we find yet another episode in the cycle of disobedience, servitude, appeal to God and rescue.

Now the Israelites were in big trouble! The Midianites, a Bedouin tribe, were like swarms of locusts; they came in their thousands and stripped the land bare. Why such an oppressive invasion? The answer is clear. 'The Israelites did evil in the eyes of the Lord' (v. 1). God needed to show them how much their wrong worship and behaviour mattered; so, for seven years he allowed (even instigated) the Midianite oppression. How sad that they had to be in such dire straits before they cried out to him for help.

And help he did – yet again. First, God sent a prophet with a clear message for them. 'I rescued you from slavery in Egypt, I gave you your land. I told you not to worship the false gods. And you have not listened.' Not listened, nor cared. There was grief as well as anger in God's message.

I was interested to learn recently that the Greek words for 'listen' and 'obey' are very similar. Their failure to do either went hand in hand. We reckon our springer spaniel had selective hearing. Whisper 'supper' and she came running; but shout 'come back' when she was chasing a rabbit and she appeared stone deaf! But are we not often the same? God nudges us to do something that seems difficult or risky and we ignore him. The devil whispers, 'Just once won't matter,' and we fall to his temptation.

Lord, I always have good intentions to obey you. But I am often distracted. Instead of listening carefully to you, I ignore you and go my own way. Please help me today to be sensitive to every nudge you give. Amen

ROSEMARY GREEN

I'm not important

'Pardon me, my lord,' Gideon replied, 'but how can I save Israel? My clan is the weakest in Manasseh, and I am the least in my family.' The Lord answered, 'I will be with you, and you will strike down all the Midianites, leaving none alive.' (NIV)

'Why?' asks the six-year-old, wanting to find out about the world around him, about the universe, about the invisible God. 'Why?' asks the adult with cancer or watching pictures of human misery on TV. 'Why has all this happened to us?' asked Gideon. 'Why has the God who rescued us from Egypt abandoned us now?' Most of the time we do not get a specific answer because we are not asking the right question. Even if we cannot make sense of the suffering, instead of asking 'Why?' our question can be, 'Lord, how do you want me to show that I trust you?'

That is the unasked question to which Gideon was given an answer. 'Go in the strength you have and save Israel.' His comment is predictable! 'But I'm a nobody.' The Lord's reply, 'I will be with you,' basically means: 'It doesn't matter who you are; what matters is who I am.'

Many, many times in scripture we read God saying, 'Don't be afraid, for I am with you.' I like putting together Jesus' words to the disciples, 'Apart from me you can do nothing' (John 15:5) with Paul's 'I can do all this through him who gives me strength' (Philippians 4:13).

Whatever our status in the world, it is a level playing field. Without God, useless; with God, powerful. We can partner the humility of admitting powerlessness with our confidence in his strength – provided, of course, that we're following his path.

Gideon's next words were ones of common ancient Near Eastern hospitality: 'Have something to eat before you leave.' His preparation of meat and unleavened bread took time, but it led to a remarkable demonstration of God's presence and power.

God is seen in unexpected and powerful ways. But often he shows himself in small, quiet ways – through the Bible, through another person, through the world around us. Let's pray that we are both observant and obedient.

ROSEMARY GREEN

Be bold for God

Joash replied to the hostile crowd around him, 'Are you going to plead Baal's cause? Are you trying to save him? Whoever fights for him shall be put to death by morning! If Baal really is a god, he can defend himself when someone breaks down his altar.' (NIV)

Are you prone to take the line of least resistance and follow the crowd? Or are you prepared to stick your neck out for Jesus and his ways, even if it is costly? Joash, Gideon's father, had followed the prevailing culture and built an altar to Baal, in direct opposition to God's explicit command, 'No other gods before me… No idols.'

Gideon, on the other hand, had already built an altar to the Lord (v. 24). Then he clearly heard some divine instructions. 'Cut down the Asherah pole (a wooden statue of a Canaanite mother-goddess) and use the wood to sacrifice your father's second-best bull.'

Not surprisingly, Gideon was afraid to stir up the wrath of both his father and the local inhabitants, so he executed God's orders under cover of darkness, with others to help. In the morning, the villagers were furious and threatened to kill him. But his father surprised him. Perhaps Joash had been secretly ashamed of his cowardice and his infidelity to the Lord. Now, emboldened by his son's example, he took a clear stand and defended both his son and his God.

Recently I visited another church member in hospital. Before I left, I wimped out of suggesting we pray together in the ward. My excuse: she might be embarrassed in front of other patients or the nurses. The truth: I was the one who feared the embarrassment. Think of some of the situations this past week when you could have spoken up for the Lord: at work, at home, at the school gate, with your leisure group, over a cuppa, in a chance encounter. What did you say? Pray that God uses your godly words, however few. Or pray for forgiveness for your failure and for greater courage next time.

I pray that today I may overcome my cowardice and be alert to opportunities to speak up and witness for you. May my actions, my words and my manner work together to make you clear and attractive. Amen

ROSEMARY GREEN

Checking it out

Gideon said to God, 'If you will save Israel by my hand as you have promised – look, I will place a wool fleece on the threshing-floor. If there is dew only on the fleece and all the ground is dry, then I will know that you will save Israel by my hand.' (NIV)

Gideon's uncertainty rings true with many of us. We often find it hard to discern God's leading. Sometimes I am too hesitant to move forward. At other times I charge ahead without checking whether my action is God's idea or just my own enthusiasm. But a real desire to obey him, partnered with a humble prayer, 'Lord, please stop me if I'm getting it wrong,' saves us from too many mistakes.

Gideon's marching orders were clear: 'Go in the strength you have and save Israel out of Midian's hand. Am I not sending you?' (v. 14). He had seen the demonstration of God's power in the fire that consumed the meat and in his meeting with the angel. He had received unexpected backing from his father, been filled with the Holy Spirit and had enlisted an army. But he still had cold feet.

Does that scenario feel familiar? Circumstances all appear to fit together, but I can still wonder whether I really ought to move forward. Gideon wanted to be sure. I used to think he was checking out God's power. Now I think it was more his own uncertainty of hearing God right.

Despite his increasing boldness, there was still an element of 'little me' in Gideon. He wanted to be quite sure that the Lord really wanted him as a leader. So, 'If the fleece is wet and the ground dry, then I'll know that you want to use me to defeat the Midianites.' In the morning the fleece was sodden, the ground dry. But he still needed further reassurance. 'Just once more, Lord. Please, a dry fleece, and wet ground.' God understood Gideon's caution and was wonderfully patient with him – just as he is often more patient with me than I deserve.

Pray: 'Thank you, Lord, for your patience with me. Please make your way clear, as far as I need, that I may step out in faith and obedience.' Now talk to him about your problems; wait to listen – and trust him to guide.

ROSEMARY GREEN

Too many by far!

The Lord said to Gideon, 'You have too many men. I cannot deliver Midian into their hands, or Israel would boast against me, "My own strength has saved me."' (NIV)

When I was a university student, the Christian group to which I belonged held its triennial evangelistic mission with a week of intense activity. We put immense energy, time and resources into this effort to encourage other students to become Christians. And we took as our motto Zechariah 4:6. '"Not by might, nor by power, but by my Spirit," says the Lord Almighty.' We needed to remember that, however diligent our efforts, no one would turn to Christ unless God's Spirit drew them. Our prayer was more important than our activity.

The story of Gideon's need to prune his army reminds me of that verse. They were not to rely on their numbers or on their own strength, but on God. Fear was the first pruning tool. God used it to reduce the army from 32,000 to 10,000, as two-thirds of the men pulled back. Fear is as prevalent now as it was then, and it is often Satan's weapon to reduce our effectiveness as Christians. We ignore the power of the Spirit when we see ourselves as strong and independent. We also leave God's power out of the reckoning when we see ourselves as weak and other people as strong, ready to mock and defeat us.

But Gideon's army was still too big. So God used another tool to reduce it – shrewdness and caution. The large majority, desperate to quench their thirst, rashly got on their knees to drink, making themselves vulnerable to attack. They were sent home. The wiser men, equally thirsty but more careful, stayed standing and bent over to get water in their hands. This enabled them to lap from their hands and stay on guard for enemy assailants. They were allowed to stay.

Reflect on Ephesians 1:18–19, where Paul prays that the Ephesians may know Christ's power. That same power which raised Jesus from the dead is available to you and me!

ROSEMARY GREEN

The big victory

'Get up! The Lord has given the Midianite camp into your hands.' Dividing the three hundred men into three companies, [Gideon] placed trumpets and empty jars in the hands of all of them, with torches inside. 'Watch me,' he told them. 'Follow my lead.' (NIV)

They say that no good comes out of eavesdropping, but that was not true for Gideon! The Lord recognised that he was still afraid of attacking the Midianite horde with his tiny army. 'If you are afraid to attack…' (v. 10). God always knows our innermost thoughts; do you find that scary or encouraging? Scripture often tells us, 'Do not be afraid, for I am with you'; or in other words, 'Don't be afraid; I've got things under control.'

So Gideon and his servant sneaked into the Midianite camp, and heard just what he needed: 'This must be the sword of Gideon.' I like his immediate reaction of worship. Am I always as ready as he was to recognise God's hand and to express my immediate thanks?

Gideon's fear now gave way to confidence, sure of his God and of victory to come. He had a clear plan to use his tiny army (300 men against 135,000; see 8:10). He was shrewd in his timing, 'at the start of the middle watch', 10.00 pm. It was dark. The first shift was tired, the new shift probably not wholly awake. No one expected trouble. As Gideon's men surrounded the camp, they broke their jars, shone their lights, blew their trumpets and shouted for the Lord. There was utter confusion. The Midianites who didn't kill one another fled in panic and were routed.

What gave Gideon's army this amazing victory? Assurance that God was with them, trustworthy leadership, team strategy and surprise were among the factors. Each one of us faces a different 'enemy'. It may be a particular individual, a difficult situation at work or at home, or our internal conflicts and temptations. Confidence in the Lord's presence and our willingness to obey him are prime factors on the path to victory.

Lord, I pray that my confidence may be in you, not in my own abilities. Help me to listen to you, to recognise your nudge and to move forward (or to wait) in faith and obedience.

ROSEMARY GREEN

The aftermath

'I will not rule over you, nor will my son rule over you. The Lord will rule over you'… Gideon made the gold into an ephod, which he placed in Ophrah, his town. All Israel prostituted themselves by worshipping it there, and it became a snare to Gideon and his family. (NIV)

This chapter is a sad end to the story of Gideon, but it still has much to teach us.

First, we find a resentful tribe. The Ephraimites felt marginalised when Gideon called the Israelites to fight the Midianites (v. 1). 'Why didn't you include us?' But Gideon's answer, acknowledging their vital contribution in the victory (vv. 2–3), reminds me of Proverbs 15:1, 'A gentle answer turns away wrath.' But Proverbs 15:1 continues, 'but a harsh word stirs up anger.'

The harsh words of the inhabitants of Sukkoth and Peniel (vv. 6–8) stirred up Gideon's fury. His reaction was excessive and vengeful. He was equally vindictive against the kings Zebah and Zalmunna, who had killed his brothers. So this chapter makes me consider how I react towards those who attack either me or the people I care about. Do I share Gideon's peace-making reply to the Ephraimites or his hot-headed violence against Sukkoth, Peniel and the Midianite kings?

Worse was to come for Gideon. Beware the slippery slope of experience! Many mighty leaders in the Old Testament deteriorated at the end of their lives or careers and it also happens today. I know of one 70-year-old who was a respected elder in his church and often travelled overseas on business. He recently confessed to his wife his numerous sexual affairs and a four-year-old son in Africa. Now he is divorced, and he has brought the boy and his mother to live with him in his own country.

Gideon, too, deteriorated spiritually after initially following God faithfully. After refusing to be made king, pointing the people back to God, he led them astray by asking them to contribute to a gold ephod, which became an object of false worship and deflected the Israelites from dedication to the Lord. A sorry end for a mighty man.

In what ways are your spirituality and your character growing more like Jesus, or declining?

ROSEMARY GREEN

What the Bible says about money

Alianore Smith writes:

Sixteen of Jesus' 38 parables and a tenth of New Testament verses deal with money. The Bible offers about 500 verses on prayer, fewer than 500 on faith and over 2,000 on money.

The Bible tells us that money – and particularly our attitude towards money – is important. It tells us that money, like all things, comes from God. But it also says that money is fleeting, and it holds no eternal value.

Money is presented to us as a tool for life on earth, but – like so much in the world – we are far too good at letting the tool master us, rather than mastering the tool ourselves. We are quick to seek after money and riches, to bow to greed and a continually growing need for 'more' rather than investing in contentment, building up heavenly treasure and seeking an eternal currency. Why is this?

There are no doubt many reasons – we are fallen, broken people. It is far easier to worship something we can see and (at least in part) control, than something we cannot see and cannot control.

Maybe when it comes to money – whether consciously or sub-consciously – we have fallen into the trap of believing that wealth is a sign of God's blessing. If you are rich, it means God favours you. If you are poor, it means he doesn't.

Of course, we are right to thank God for the blessings in our lives. But it seems to me that I, at least, am very good at acknowledging that God gives good gifts, but I'm less good at acknowledging that he takes them away… and that either way, I should still be saying, with Job: 'May the name of the Lord be praised' (Job 1:21, NIV).

Over the next fortnight, we're going to explore some of what the Bible says about money. We shall realise that it is not money itself that is bad or dangerous, but our attitude towards it can be. Our love of money, our overinflated sense of its worth and its power, our misguided belief that we can control it… it is there that the danger lies, and it is that against which we are warned.

So as we consider wealth, riches, poverty and eternal significance, let us remember this: the Lord gives, and the Lord takes away. Blessed be the name of the Lord.

A Christmas surprise

The earth is the Lord's, and everything in it, the world, and all who live in it; for he founded it on the seas and established it on the waters. (NIV)

Every Christmas she would do the same thing. Throughout December, she'd sneak into her little brother's room while he was out and take one or two items. Storing them under her bed, on Christmas Eve she would wrap them, label them, sign them and put them under the tree. 'To Ben, love Emily', they would say.

And every Christmas it would be the same – utter confusion from her little brother as he unwrapped a present from his sister… and realised that it was something he *already had*. In fact, it wasn't just a duplicate of something he already had, it was something that was his in the first place.

We all know that it is nothing short of rude to give as a gift something that already belongs to the recipient – it is stingy, and it is mean.

And yet, when we think about giving of ourselves, our possessions and our finances to God, that is exactly what we find ourselves doing. This psalm makes clear that everything in and on the earth belongs to God – from the people and the animals themselves right through to the money and goods that change hands on a daily basis. Everything we have comes from God, and *he* is the rightful owner… he's just lent it to us!

As we start to think about how we as Christians should view, spend and use our money, this is a helpful place to start: the earth is the Lord's, and everything in it. Giving what we have back to him is not the selfish move of a sneaky big sister at Christmas, but instead an honouring of what has first been given to us.

It's a difficult starting point to get our heads around, but an incredibly freeing one when we do.

Father, thank you for your abundant generosity to us in sharing all that you have with us. Please teach us to change our perspective and view our possessions not as 'ours' but as a gift from you. Amen

ALIANORE SMITH

When truth offends

'Yours, Lord, is the greatness and the power and the glory and the majesty and the splendour, for everything in heaven and earth is yours. Yours, Lord, is the kingdom; you are exalted as head over all. Wealth and honour come from you; you are the ruler of all things.' (NIV)

David's prayer in 1 Chronicles 29 is in equal measure offensive and freeing. It's offensive because we like to think that what we have, we earned. The world tells us that we've earned it, so we can keep it. We can do with it what we want. But this passage tells us the opposite. It reminds us that everything – from everlasting to everlasting – begins and ends with God. And that 'everything in heaven and earth is God's'. This is offensive.

But it is also freeing. Because if we alone have earned what we have, then we can only ever rely on ourselves to provide. The only option is to cling on to what we have, store up treasure and put stuff aside in case a rainy day comes along. To start and end with ourselves is to live in fear. But when we start and end with God and his generosity, there is freedom, humility and joy. When we realise that 'everything in heaven and on earth is God's', we are filled with a joy like that of David; we cannot help but praise.

This message may be offensive to your pride and your selfishness, but it is liberation from fear and bondage to the self. It is glorious truth. For when we start with God, we find joy instead of fear, humility instead of pride and generosity instead of selfishness.

When we fully understand the height, breadth and depth of what God has given us, we cannot help but be generous ourselves. And we can have pure joy as we do so, for we know that God has provided before and he will continue to provide, for all things come from him.

Read 1 Chronicles 29:1–20 aloud – really consider the weight and the impact of the words. Ask that God would teach you once again that all good things come from him – and he can be trusted to provide, no matter what.

ALIANORE SMITH

Do you trust me?

Those who trust in their riches will fall, but the righteous will thrive like a green leaf. (NIV)

One of my favourite videos on the internet (aside from all the ones of dogs, of course) is one where a family are trying to convince their son to do the 'do you trust me?' fall back into their arms. He is standing on a chair and they are gathered behind him with their arms out. After a short hesitation, he closes his eyes, takes a deep breath and… falls forward, away from the people waiting to catch him.

This passage in Proverbs always reminds me of that video. To trust in riches, Proverbs says, is to fall in the exact opposite direction to where safety lies. Because you cannot trust your life to more than one thing; it is either God or money in whom we must put our ultimate trust.

That's not to say that Proverbs has anything against riches – in other places of the book, it suggests that wealth can be a blessing from God for wise behaviour (see 3:9–10; 10:22). But although riches can be a blessing, they do not offer protection from the evils of the world. They hold very little power in the battle against death and destruction. Righteousness and a fear of the Lord are where we should put our trust.

I wonder, which way do you fall in a crisis? Do you fall forward, into the thin air of imagined protection given by what money can buy? Or do you fall backward in trust that underneath are the everlasting arms, and righteousness – his and yours – will not only catch you but also help you to thrive in this strange old world?

Father God, teach me to put my trust in you and you alone – not riches and wealth, not what money can buy me, but purely your everlasting arms. Amen
ALIANORE SMITH

Tithing

'A tithe of everything from the land, whether grain from the soil or fruit from the trees, belongs to the Lord; it is holy to the Lord… Every tithe of the herd and flock – every tenth animal that passes under the shepherd's rod – will be holy to the Lord.' (NIV)

If you are not an owner of land or livestock, this passage may feel a little irrelevant and perhaps even outdated. What could it possibly have to do with our attitude to money today? How can a sheep 'be holy to the Lord'? Do I have to bless every fifth lamb chop I buy, and eat it? What does this really look like today?

To consider tithing in today's world is to consider what it means to acknowledge that everything we have is God's. To tithe is to give back to God before we do anything else, to give of our 'first fruits' and to express – not only with our words but also with our actions– that our trust is in him.

The Mosaic laws are pretty prescriptive about the nature of tithing for the Israelites, but today, different people do tithing differently. Some give ten percent of their pre-tax income, some of their post-tax income. Others give a different percentage. Some see tithing as giving directly to their local church; others split their giving between church, charities and other needs. One friend of mine keeps aside a certain amount each month for random acts of generosity, so, she says, she never has an excuse to walk past someone in need.

I don't think we should be legalistic about this. Tithing is an act of worship – it shows gratitude to God for his provisions. It is also an act of love, of giving out of love for others to the work of the gospel in the world – whether that is through proclamation of the gospel or mercy ministries.

What matters, as ever, is the attitude of the heart as we give.

This week, take a look through your financial outgoings and spend some time in prayer, asking God where you can give from your 'first fruits' and not just your leftovers.

ALIANORE SMITH

Debt and dignity

Do not charge a fellow Israelite interest, whether on money or food or anything else that may earn interest. (NIV)

As someone who started university after 2012, I am in the group of people who paid £9,000 for their fees – plus loans for living costs. This means that when I left university, I had over £30,000 worth of debt. At the time of writing, this debt has increased to over £47,000. Each month, I accrue nearly £200 worth of interest, while only paying back about £11.

You can see why this passage makes me wish our society operated by the Deuteronomic laws.

Let's be honest though – these laws weren't written for 21st-century recipients of government educational loans. This is about lending within a community, about informal, personal loans, about generosity to the poor and needy, and it comes within the context of a whole bunch of other laws about gleaning, tithing and distributing produce to those who were without.

And there are many things that can be said about all those details. But for now, let's focus on loans.

The thing about lending to those in your community who find themselves in need of it, you see, is that it bestows dignity upon the recipient. Almsgiving – or charity – was in place for those in financial need who could not pay back a loan, but for those who found themselves with a pressing financial need and had the power to pay it back, a loan is a way to affirm dignity and avoid the potential for dependency.

And, of course, a gift to charity can be given only once – a loan can be gifted over and over again to different people when they are in need.

As we hold our money lightly, and seek to bless those who are less fortunate than us, what might it look like today to consider loans *as well as* almsgiving and charity donations?

Father, teach me today to hold my disposable income lightly. Give me eyes to see those in need and prompt me to bestow dignity as well as show generosity to those in need. Amen

ALIANORE SMITH

Who are the rich?

Look! The wages you failed to pay the workers who mowed your fields are crying out against you. The cries of the harvesters have reached the ears of the Lord Almighty. You have lived on earth in luxury and self-indulgence. (NIV)

The question that James is posing for us here is simple: if you are rich, how are you using your money?

You see, if you have food in your fridge, clothes on your back, a roof over your head and a place to sleep, then you are richer than 75% of the world. If you have money in the bank, in your wallet and some spare change, you are among the top eight percent of the world's wealthy.

We are the rich, and that means we have a responsibility. And even if we don't run businesses, we still have workers.

Are you wearing clothes? Did you pick the cotton that makes them? Did you sew the items yourself? No? Then someone else did. Are you sipping your morning mug of tea or coffee? Did you pick the leaves or beans yourself? Did you grind and package it? No? Then someone else did.

These people – these people who picked your cotton and sewed your clothes, who grew and harvested your coffee beans – are they being paid a fair wage? Are they earning enough to survive and to support themselves and their families? I couldn't tell you if that was the case for the clothes I'm wearing right now, or the tea I'm sipping as I write these words. But I should be able to.

Just because we now live in a globalised culture and we cannot see the workers who provide our goods does not mean we have less of a duty to care for them. They are our global neighbours. Do not compromise on justice just to save money. Do not sacrifice someone else's livelihood for a bargain. If we do, we are no better than the rich oppressors to whom James is writing.

Father, teach me to care about those workers whose toil has resulted in the things I own and benefit from. Teach me generosity, teach me to love well – give me courage and kindness in my convictions and with my wealth. Amen

ALIANORE SMITH

(Un)certain riches

Command those who are rich in this present world not to be arrogant nor to put their hope in wealth, which is so uncertain, but to put their hope in God, who richly provides us with everything for our enjoyment. (NIV)

What is the most valuable thing you own? For me, it's my engagement ring, given to me by my fiancé in Richmond Park on a crisp January afternoon.

And yet Paul, writing to Timothy in this passage, makes clear that although valuable, my ring – or indeed, anything material this world has to give – should not be my most precious possession. Ultimately, it offers me nothing. It represents a promise, yes. It reminds me of my fiancé (now husband) and our love for each other, yes. It is beautiful, yes. But I cannot stake my life on it; it will not protect me from the brokenness of the world. It will not come with me when I die, and it offers me no real security.

This is the point that Paul is making about riches: they are uncertain. They offer us no real security and we should not put our hope in them. Instead, we must acknowledge, as Job 1:21 does, that 'naked I came from my mother's womb, and naked I shall depart'. It may be tempting to gather and hoard and use possessions and wealth to cushion ourselves against the brokenness of the world but, in the end, they will do nothing to help us.

It is God, Paul writes to Timothy, who provides us with everything we need. Not our wealth, not our possessions, not our aspirations and our dreams… but God. Riches can be here today and gone tomorrow, but God is faithful 'from generation to generation'. His character, his presence and his promises remain sure and certain no matter what.

And it is there – on the character and promises of God, rather than shiny objects or full bank accounts – that we must stake our hope.

God, sometimes the world is loud, and the comfort offered by riches is more tempting than I can bear. Teach me to stake my hope on that which is lasting and secure, and seek you and you alone. Amen

ALIANORE SMITH

Simon says...

Peter answered: 'May your money perish with you, because you thought you could buy the gift of God with money! You have no part or share in this ministry, because your heart is not right before God.' (NIV)

The word 'simony' – the buying or selling of ecclesiastical privileges (offices, pardons, benefices) – comes from this story. The idea that you can buy positions of power in the church – or indeed the love of God – should shock us.

Of course, it's easy to read this story and think to ourselves, 'Silly Simon, I would *never* seek to do something as brazenly foolish and arrogant as that!'

And yet when I read through this story, I find myself challenged. Perhaps we are appalled at this story of Simon, at the mere suggestion that one would seek to purchase God's affection and blessing with riches. But how often do we seek to purchase God's affection, approval and blessing with something other than riches? With good deeds, with penance and fasting, with self-righteousness or (emotional) self-flagellation.

When we allow God to search our hearts, do we find – somewhere in the midst of all that we see and know and believe about him – a secret belief that, somehow, we can purchase his love? That without our good deeds or our achievements, we are unworthy or unable to receive his Holy Spirit?

That belief is a pesky little weed that grows in my heart over and over again. I uproot it time and again, but still it beds down and rears its ugly head at the most inopportune moments.

And so, as much as we may wish to judge, condemn or reflect with horror on what Simon did, we must also acknowledge that – more often than not – we are no better.

But God is faithful, he is kind and he is true. And he gives his love and his Spirit willingly to those who ask for it.

Search my heart, O God, and show me where beliefs of my ability to purchase or earn your love have taken root. Teach me of your kindness and grace. Restore to me a new understanding of your love – free to all who ask. Amen

ALIANORE SMITH

Leftovers and folly

Then he said to them, 'Watch out! Be on your guard against all kinds of greed; life does not consist in an abundance of possessions.' (NIV)

Picture the scene: you've hosted a dinner party, and you have more leftovers than you expected. It's late at night and the food is going to go off if you don't do something with it. Your freezer is full. What do you do?

This is the kind of situation in which the rich fool found himself… except he doesn't just seek to borrow a neighbour's freezer space; he goes out to buy a second freezer. This is not as foolish as we often think. This farmer had an abundant harvest, and he needed to store his grain safely to stop it from spoiling. To build bigger barns was not, in fact, a ridiculous idea.

And it's worth noting that Jesus doesn't condemn him for his plans. Jesus points out that the rich man's folly lies not in what he does but in what he fails to consider. He fails to consider that the end of his earthly life may come sooner than he anticipated and, were that to happen, he would lose all that he had worked for, because he had worked only for earthly riches and not been 'rich towards God'.

God does not condemn us for being good stewards of what we have been given on earth – crops or finances or anything else – but he does condemn greed. He condemns the attitude that our life consists only of an abundance of possessions, an assumption that the more we have, the happier we will be (this is the attitude of the man who asks Jesus to tell his brother to divide the inheritance with him).

Possessions and riches may be useful, but they offer no lasting security in the eternal scheme of things. So, continue to steward well what you have, but be on your guard against 'all kinds of greed'.

Where in your life might you be running the risk of putting hope in material possessions or riches? Take some time to bring this to God in prayer, asking for an eternal perspective.

ALIANORE SMITH

'My precious…'

'Do not store up for yourselves treasures on earth, where moths and vermin destroy, and where thieves break in and steal. But store up for yourselves treasures in heaven… where thieves do not break in and steal. For where your treasure is, there your heart will be also.' (NIV)

'Suddenly, Gollum sat down and began to weep, a whistling and gurgling sound horrible to listen to.' This line from *The Hobbit* by J.R.R. Tolkien is written as Gollum realises that the ring has been taken from him. It seems to me that Gollum is a good example of someone whose heart is where their treasure is. For Gollum, the ring is 'my precious' treasure. For us… well, it could be anything. What do we consider precious? To what do we align our hearts?

When my mum's home was burgled on her 18th birthday, her father quoted this verse at her. As you can imagine, it didn't go down particularly well at the time. But when you have been a victim of 20+ burglaries in 15 years (as my mother was growing up), this verse takes on a whole new level of meaning. And, 35 years later, she tells the story of her father's words as one which formed her in an unexpected way.

It's worth noting, of course, that the passage that follows this is the famous 'do not worry' instruction of Jesus. And that rings true – if we serve possessions and money as master, we have only ourselves to rely on. But if we serve God – the maker of the universe, the giver of all good gifts – then we are relying not on ourselves but on the one who loved us so much that he gave his very life to save us.

I would perhaps avoid quoting this passage at someone who has just been burgled on their 18th birthday, but the truth remains nonetheless: wealth on earth is fleeting. God's provision endures forever.

Listen to the song 'All I Once Held Dear'. Reflect on the words and consider them in the light of this passage. Talk to God about your attitude towards money, where your heart is and where you wish it to be.

ALIANORE SMITH

Boiled sweets

'They all gave out of their wealth; but she, out of her poverty, put in everything – all she had to live on.' (NIV)

A modern-day widow's mite:

It was a normal Sunday, sometime in 2011, the 6.00 pm service at church. As usual, during the final hymn a bag was passed round for donations to the work of the church. It was my job to count the money. As always, I tipped the bag upside down and let the coins, notes and envelopes fall out on to the desk.

Except that this week there was something different. In among all the shiny coins and slightly crumpled notes, there lay a solitary boiled sweet – a reddish-brown colour, wrapped in crispy, crinkly cellophane. I laughed it off, brushing it aside as a joke, a mistake, a moment of madness by a visiting eccentric.

I counted the money and dutifully noted the addition of the boiled sweet at the bottom of the collection sheet. Over dinner that evening I mentioned the boiled sweet to my mum, the vicar, recounting it as a funny story.

I didn't get the laugh I was expecting.

'Yes,' she said quietly, 'I know about that. One of the ladies approached me at the end of the service this evening. She told me that her benefits ran out on Friday and she hasn't been able to afford food for the weekend, so she's been living on boiled sweets. When she heard that the offering would be used to help the work of the church, she knew she didn't have any money, so she decided that she would give up her final boiled sweet instead.'

This woman gave more than was required of her. She gave at great personal cost. Out of her poverty, she gave all she had to live on.

Today, what might it look like for you to give away your last boiled sweet?

ALIANORE SMITH

Cheerfully given

Remember this: whoever sows sparingly will also reap sparingly, and whoever sows generously will also reap generously. Each of you should give what you have decided in your heart to give, not reluctantly or under compulsion, for God loves a cheerful giver. (NIV)

Why do we give? For the ancients at the time Paul was writing, people's motive for giving was to show one's moral superiority. Sometimes, we give because we feel obliged to, or because we would feel guilty if we didn't. Maybe we are generous because that's how we've been brought up. Maybe we're generous because we're scared that God will be cross with us if we aren't.

There are many reasons – good and bad – that we might give and be generous. Paul, in contrast to the ancients at the time he was writing, says that our motive for giving should be to glorify God for his grace.

It is important, of course, to state that this is not about sneakily getting in a works-based righteousness. Paul is not saying that God *only* loves you *if* you are a cheerful giver, and if you don't give or you don't give cheerfully, he doesn't love you. The act of giving to others does not earn God's blessing or his favour.

Instead, what Paul is saying is that giving to others is a practical outworking of trusting in God's promises. Human righteousness – which includes giving generously – owes its existence to and is an expression of God's righteousness. To give generously to another is to show a little of God's generosity to you, and to declare your reliance on his goodness and his provision throughout your life.

So why do we give? Not out of obligation, not out of guilt, not out of fear – but out of delight and trust in the God who has freely given to us and who will wonderfully supply all our needs.

Next time you are giving something away – money, time, emotional energy – check your motives. Take a moment to thank God that because he freely gives to you, you are able to do the same for others.

ALIANORE SMITH

Test your limits

Jesus answered, 'If you want to be perfect, go, sell your possessions and give to the poor, and you will have treasure in heaven. Then come, follow me.' When the young man heard this, he went away sad, because he had great wealth. (NIV)

What is your limit? What's the line you would not cross, even if God himself asked you to? What would you refuse to give up? What would you refuse to do?

As a 'good Christian woman', my immediate answer is: 'Nothing at all, of course; I would give up anything Jesus asked me to!' But when I dig a little deeper and am a little more honest with myself, I find my limit. I know what I would find it near impossible to give up, even if God asked me to.

This is the conundrum faced by the rich young man in this passage. This man who tries so hard to do all that is right, to earn the rewards of eternal life, is confronted with a choice: will you give up the thing(s) you hold most dear in order to follow me?

Tom Wright, in his book *Matthew for Everyone*, writes this: 'With this young man, he [Jesus] sensed that his possessions had become his idol, his alternative god, the demon that would eventually kill him unless he renounced it.'

It is easy to read this passage as an instruction to sell everything we have or to feel guilty for not doing so. But maybe this passage is more nuanced than that. Maybe we should see this passage as an opportunity to take an honest look, once again, at ourselves.

What is it that, if God asked us to give it up, we would not be able to let go of? What is it that has such a firm grip on our hearts, such a rootedness in our identity, that to give it up in the service of God would be just too much to ask?

Those things are what we need to learn to surrender today.

Father, some things feel too big, too comfortable and too safe for me to give up, even for you. Would you teach me once again of your character, your faithfulness and your call, so that I can once again learn to trust in you? Amen
ALIANORE SMITH

What's your bass line?

**I know what it is to be in need, and I know what it is to have plenty.
I have learned the secret of being content in any and every situation,
whether well fed or hungry, whether living in plenty or in want. (NIV)**

You know Pachelbel's Canon? It's a delightful piece of music – unless you're a cellist. If you're a cellist, all you play in Pachelbel's Canon is eight repeating notes. Over and over again for nearly seven minutes. Over the top, played by the violins, is the beautiful melody that everyone knows so well, with varying notes and extravagant embellishments.

Nobody really pays attention to the work of the cellists in Pachelbel's Canon, down on the bass line. But without them, the whole piece falls apart.

Sometimes, I find life is like the violins in Pachelbel's Canon. Our emotions – happiness, sadness, despair, anger, disappointment, excitement, anticipation – are the exciting embellishments that you pay the most attention to on a day-to-day basis. But what's your bass line?

There has to be an underpinning to the melody of our lives, something that just keeps going, no matter the pitch, speed or intensity of what goes on around us.

In this passage, Paul says that his bass line is contentment.

Contentment is not to be confused with happiness. Happiness is transient; happiness is the changeable melody dependent on circumstances. Happiness is the violins. But contentment? Contentment is unchangeable. It is learnt the hard way. And it is the gift of God.

To be content with riches or poverty, in hunger or in fullness, in every situation: *that* is the bass line of a disciple of Jesus.

So stop for a minute and listen to the bass line of your life. Strain your ears past the melody of your day-to-day emotion and listen to what underpins all that you do. If your bass line springs from the one who brings peace and fulfilment to all who know him, no matter what, then it will continue even when any other music fades. And that is true contentment.

God, would you teach me the bass line of contentment – no matter where or in what situation I find myself. Amen

ALIANORE SMITH

Jesus, the storyteller

Bridget Plass writes:

Like many of you, I grew up with the stories Jesus told. Picture-book stories. No nasty bits. Happy endings. But as an adult, like lots of others, I have come to recognise not only the skill of the storyteller, but also the fact that the stories were never aimed at children. Many of the truths that Jesus slipped in are as challenging now as they were then, and are capable of making this reader, at least, extremely uncomfortable.

One thing that struck me this time round was that all the stories were told within a specific context. The wider context was, of course, that everyone was subject to the superpower that was Rome, as well as living under the heavy hand of Jewish law. The precise context was created by the immediate situation of the people to whom the stories were addressed. Tone and content were equally relevant: sometimes stark and uncompromising, sometimes full of love and wit and light, sometimes tongue-in-cheek and sometimes challenging the status quo.

These notes, written in the context of months of compulsory lockdown, inevitably include some things I have learnt and reflected on during that period. I think I have once again been amazed at how relevant these stories are to current experiences, even if the allusions are foreign to us. Perhaps for the first time in the developed western world we have been faced with an awareness that, however advanced, science does not have an immediate answer to such afflictions as this killer virus.

All over the world rules became tougher. Even when the intention was to protect, the result was multifaceted: loneliness, abuse of power, anger, confusion, exploitation, despair. And right in our faces on a daily basis were the latest devastating figures of those suffering and those mourning the death of people they love.

Poverty may be relative when contrasted to the time of Jesus, but the fear related to losing employment or a self-made business has been the same for many people attempting to live through the pandemic. Our experiences would have resonated with people living precariously in the towns and villages which Jesus visited, and hopefully our new understanding will breathe even more life into the parables I have chosen.

The wise and foolish builders

'Everyone who hears these words of mine and does not put them into practice is like a foolish man who built his house on sand. The rain came down, the streams rose, and the winds blew and beat against that house, and it fell with a great crash.' (NIV)

Such a cosy children's story. Silly old builder who built his house on the sand. We all know what happens to sandcastles when the tide comes in. But we grown-ups in our western, established faith structures were different – built on as solid foundations as the buildings we worshipped in.

Then in 2020, something happened that was as ruthless and frightening as a tidal wave, and all of us experienced the devastation of the familiar, which many who have been bereaved or abandoned have already experienced. Suddenly the safe, solid structures we relied on appeared as flimsy as painted stage sets, which, when they fell flat, revealed chaos. Where was authority? Where were the answers? What was the truth? Where was God?

For some of us, it was as though everything we valued had been swept away and nothing worth having was left. Storms of fear proved overwhelming. Others of us wobbled like mad, but in solitude found we could dig deep and lay new foundations, discovering it wasn't too late to put into action the Jesus blueprint. Some of us were surprised to discover our little house was standing firm, built on a rock of actively following Jesus, and just got on with the job of seeking out and caring for the frightened, the lonely and the lost. Some of us are wishing we had been stronger.

It's never easy to start again, to face the cost of building a new solid house consisting of truth and love, but we can trust in our God of a thousand new beginnings. Unfortunately, as Jesus never tired of pointing out, it's not enough to read manuals or opt for easy; it's going to involve doing, and that will always result in aching backs and dirty hands.

Dear Father, help us today to face the truth of what we need to do to firm up our foundations. Give us the courage to turn words into actions and be part of building your kingdom. Amen

BRIDGET PLASS

The great banquet

'A certain man was preparing a great banquet and invited many guests… But they all alike began to make excuses… Then the owner of the house became angry and ordered his servant, "… Bring in the poor, the crippled, the blind and the lame… I tell you, not one of those who were invited will get a taste of my banquet."' (NIV)

During the pandemic in the UK, we witnessed the virtual creation of a new-style rich list, celebrated noisily on our doorsteps every Thursday for months. NHS staff, carers, cleaners, refuse collectors, shop assistants, delivery drivers – all became our heroes. Those of us obediently locking down even became known as 'local heroes'. And the invisible became visible: bereavement, domestic abuse, dementia, frailty, vulnerable children, poverty, cramped living, homelessness. We wanted to hear from those with close-hand experience, to know what made them tick. They became top of our lists for who we would invite to dinner.

The Black Lives Matter campaign that followed, which encouraged us to think about many occasions of extraordinary blindness and selfish treatment now and throughout history.

Jesus was there before us. From the moment he stood in the synagogue after returning from his desert trials and quoted from Isaiah, he was committed to bringing to the attention of the privileged that *all* lives matter: especially the forgotten, the outsiders and the vulnerable. And he didn't leave it there, both in the way he lived his life and in the stories he told.

Tougher still, in this story he rammed home his message that not everyone gets a happy ending. In the feast of heaven there would be no top table reserved for those who felt it was their right to sit there, but also no repeat invitations for those who considered themselves too important, busy or distracted to value the first one.

Dear Father, help me to remember today to thank you , really thank you, for my invitation to be a guest at your banquet in heaven and to never forget or take lightly how much each invitation cost you. Amen

BRIDGET PLASS

The good Samaritan

'A man was going down from Jerusalem to Jericho, when he was attacked by robbers… A priest… passed by on the other side… So too, a Levite… But a Samaritan… when he saw him, he took pity on him.' (NIV)

The highly qualified 'expert' was confident of tricking Jesus into saying something contrary to Jewish law. Jesus turns the tables by asking two questions. His first bats the ball back into his opponent's court, asking him how he reads the law. The answer is theoretically correct in every detail.

'Good stuff,' says Jesus, 'Now go and put it into practice' (or words to that effect). Expert knowledge of theory is one thing. Practical application another, especially when it involves stepping out of one's comfort zone. Attempting to divert attention, the lawyer lobs back a query about his neighbour's identity.

So familiar is the story that follows that it is easy to minimise the impact of the opening sentence: 'A man was going down from Jerusalem to Jericho.' Not so his audience. This particular road was so notorious for violent robberies that the attack on the traveller would have come as no surprise.

The response of the priest and the Levite would not, however, have had the same impact. A Jewish audience would have accepted that both, steeped in the law, were set apart from physically and practically stepping in to help. Then comes the shock denouement which we all know so well. The Samaritan, a member of the virtually untouchable race, sees, stops and does everything he can to save his oppressor's life.

Jesus asks his second question. Unwilling to affirm an alien national, the lawyer's reply is 'the one who showed mercy'. However, he will have been given some very indigestible food for thought.

During the pandemic, frantically working in intensive care, united medical staff of all faiths and none showed practical demonstrations of love that went far beyond their theoretical medical qualifications. Gender, nationality, beliefs – all irrelevant. Worth thinking about?

Today, help us remember we love only because you gave us the ability to love, that you planted seeds of love within all created beings and we should celebrate it wherever and whenever we witness it. Amen

BRIDGET PLASS

The unforgiving servant

'The kingdom of heaven is like a king who wanted to settle accounts…
A man who owed him ten thousand bags of gold was brought to him…
The servant's master took pity on him, cancelled the debt and let
him go. But when that servant went out, he found one of his fellow
servants who owed him a hundred silver coins. He grabbed him and
began to choke him.' (NIV)

The context? Peter thinks he is getting something right for once! Forgiving
three times was rabbinic teaching, while 'seven' was equivalent to using
a 'million' today to express an extremely large or unlimited quantity. The
story Jesus tells in response at first glance seems way over the top.

For starters, the servant has got into debt to the tune of 10,000 talents
('bags of gold'), impossible to pay back, bearing in mind it only cost David
3,000 talents to build an entire temple. But in our world of easy credit and
shark-like debt collecting firms with legal rights to remove everything
you possess, it is as relevant as ever, emphasising not only extraordinary
generosity on the master's part, but also great news for the servant's family, who would have potentially been up for sale to pay off the debt.

The contrast to the same servant's response to his work mate, who owes
him a tiny fraction of that sum, is dramatic enough without the shocking
conclusion of the story. Jesus says this is exactly what 'our heavenly Father'
will do to us if we fail to forgive. Why so harsh? Maybe because the servant's
behaviour symbolised what for us is a daily temptation.

We once knew a man notorious for noisily arriving incredibly late for
every church service, but who was always welcomed as if it had never
happened. One day he arrived early. When the time came for the congregation to share from the front what was on their heart, he chose to berate
the single mum who had that morning arrived breathlessly late with her
two small children in tow. Thoughtless and cruel, especially bearing in
mind the forgiving nature of the congregation towards him in the past.
Small in comparison? Maybe.

---

*Dear Father, you know exactly what is really going on inside us when faced
with the responsibility to forgive. Help us to bring more of your loving forgiveness into everything we think and do. Amen*

BRIDGET PLASS

Every picture tells a story

'Let the little children come to me… for the kingdom of God belongs to such as these…' And he took the children in his arms, placed his hands on them and blessed them.

'Truly I tell you, unless you change and become like little children, you will never enter the kingdom of heaven.' (NIV)

In 2020 it felt as though everything we knew was turned on its head and a new language was created. One phrase, ever-present as we moved slowly and sometimes painfully forward, was 'new normal', summed up for me when witnessing a happy little three-year-old playing shops with her uncle.

'Only two people are allowed in at a time. And,' she added sternly, 'you can only come in if you wear a mask.' This was what she heard every day and accepted. The image has stayed in my mind as a superb illustration of the extraordinary change that has taken place throughout the world.

Not all stories are told in words – in fact these days very few are, without the aid of some form of visual imaging. The sight of a small boy brought forward to illustrate a radical truth was a genuine 'power point'. The public encouragement of women to bring their children for Jesus to bless them another.

Yet again Jesus takes an accepted norm and turns it on its head. Bewildering to a society in which children and women had little more value than slaves, viewed as physically weak burdens with little value to the wider life of the community. Part of a new normal – a pancake flipped, God's kingdom here on earth symbolised by small children.

It seems it has always been difficult for adults to accept change to what is considered normal. Acceptance of Gentiles needed a flipping of the natural order, as did, in our lifetime, the allowing of women into church leadership. Becoming a child means inviting new ideas to enter our imaginations without fear, accepting the potential for change as a new and exciting addition to the game of life.

Dear Father, help us to grasp the possibilities of a 'now normal' today, to open our imaginations and hearts to receive the new situations and new challenges you offer us with childlike openness and wonder. Amen

BRIDGET PLASS

The lost coin

'Suppose a woman has ten silver coins and loses one. Doesn't she light a lamp, sweep the house and search carefully until she finds it?… In the same way, I tell you, there is rejoicing in the presence of the angels of God over one sinner who repents.' (NIV)

Like many others, we bought a jigsaw during last year's lockdown. It turned out to be a fiendishly difficult, thousand-piece copy of a Monet painting. Several pain-filled weeks later, 997 pieces were finally and firmly in place. Three were missing. Never has our living room been so thoroughly turned upside down. Under the carpet, down the back of the sofa, no corner was left unsearched, but sadly there was no rejoicing in our house as not even one of the three returned.

Hardly a major tragedy, but this 'lost' story is often considered equally trivial. Let's stop there. Poor, so poor there is no servant and no husband to care for her as she sweeps her dirt floor with just the light of one lamp. And a woman. To an audience traditionally consisting of men, this focus in itself is remarkable, but no more remarkable than the storyteller himself, Jesus: God made man, who turned himself into the least of the least in order to search out and save every lost soul who has rolled out of sight, and who could be lost for ever unless actively searched for.

And just as our jigsaw can never be complete without the missing pieces, so heaven cannot be complete without every single one of God's precious children. Never for our Father God the maxim 'out of sight, out of mind'. Yet how easy it is for people to roll out of our sight. To realise, for example, when hunting through addresses before sending out Christmas cards, you haven't really given some people a thought in months. That you have no idea what is happening in their lives. So, this little story punches way above its weight, doesn't it?

Dear Father, we are sorry for the times when we have been lazy. Today help us to see into the dusty corners of our memories so we can remember those we have forgotten and search them out on your behalf. Amen

BRIDGET PLASS

The lost sheep

'Suppose one of you has a hundred sheep and loses one of them. Doesn't he leave the ninety-nine in the open country and go after the lost sheep until he finds it? And when he finds it, he joyfully puts it on his shoulders and goes home. Then he calls his friends and neighbours together and says, "Rejoice with me; I have found my lost sheep."' (NIV)

I sometimes wish I had never seen a children's version of this story: the sheep depicted as adorably mischievous, curly-lashed eyes brimming with tears, tangled in a thorn bush. I have never met a grown sheep that looks anything like that, and the focus of the story was never intended to be about the qualities of the sheep but the shepherd.

Shepherding was and is always about daily intensive care, with the health and safety of the whole flock their responsibility. Again and again through the Old Testament, we hear God, through his prophets, warning about lazy shepherds who have ill-treated their sheep, haven't kept them safe from danger or bothered to look for them when they got lost.

On speaking engagement tours with my husband, we often encouraged others to support a children's charity, laying out pictures of children to be sponsored. Almost always left unchosen on the table are the least attractive ones, sometimes glaring, often teenagers. In a world where we place so much value on how people look and sound, maybe we need reminding of our responsibility to those who have little to smile about.

Our churches are supposed to offer the safety of the sheep pen. Yet if someone suddenly disappears without explanation or storms off hurt and angry, it's tempting to let them go without facing whether we have neglected them or even abused them in some way.

Yet we claim to represent the good shepherd himself, who loves and values each one of us so much that, as the story demonstrates, he would risk all to rescue us from danger and lead us to safety – which is exactly what he did 2,000 years ago, dying in the process.

Dear Father, forgive us for every time our actions, words or neglect have caused any of your precious sheep to leave the safety of the fold. Help us to find the courage and humility to search again. Amen

BRIDGET PLASS

Wise or foolish?

'The kingdom of heaven will be like ten virgins who took their lamps and went out to meet the bridegroom… The foolish ones took their lamps but did not take any oil with them. The wise ones, however, took oil in jars along with their lamps.' (NIV)

So here's the question. Should the sensible bridesmaids have shared their oil with the silly ones? When young, and being of the Mary rather than Martha variety, I would definitely have said yes.

Have you ever run out of petrol? Convinced yourself that you have just about enough to get to the next service station? Faced the humiliation of the undignified long petrol-can walk? I have! I'm afraid I would have been one of those trotting probably miles to buy oil, getting back only to find the door slammed shut. Devastated to hear the celebrations through a locked door and knowing they had not only failed the bridegroom, but also lost out themselves.

I realise now that the decision they made was based on not wanting to risk letting the bridegroom down. After all, he was the key player at his wedding! Sadly, I also know it's miserable when we feel we've let God down: to be aware we are missing out, to end up dry and empty, having run out of spiritual fuel.

We learnt a lot about looking out for each other during lockdown, making sure our neighbours didn't run out of what they needed while, in locking down ourselves, trying to support those who had a key role at that time.

Perhaps this story is a reminder that we need to keep a closer eye on those we see in danger of running out of faith and hope, before they give up and eventually even become in danger of missing the promised celebrations. And remind others and ourselves that Jesus told us we can always come to him to be topped up with living water.

Dear Father, show us who is in danger right now. Help us to top them up with love and encouragement, and point them in the direction of the one and only source of dependable love before it's too late. Amen

BRIDGET PLASS

The sower and the seed

'A farmer went out to sow his seed… Some fell along the path… Some fell on rocky places… The plants… withered because they had no root. Other seed fell among thorns, which grew up and choked the plants. Still other seed fell on good soil.' (NIV)

This is one of the only stories Jesus takes time to unpack, which is ironic as I confess I have always felt that it seems very unfair. Having worked with children in the care system for many years and known, loved and frequently respected many adults who have grown up in appalling circumstances, it is difficult to accept that it is simply tough luck if the soil you landed in, through no fault of your own, makes it very hard for the truth of the gospel to take root: thorny, rocky, nutrient-lacking soil offering little or no shade.

But we know that Jesus never ever told a story that he didn't intend to impact on the lives of those who heard it, and that means us. We cannot just 'tut tut' and shake our heads over the sadness of the glaring truth that not all people are in a position to joyfully receive the good news, any more than we can assume our runner beans will thrive if they are never watered and left to struggle through tangles of weeds and stones.

We are called by Jesus to work for as long as it takes to change the situation of the most fragile and ailing human seedlings, breaking through rock, battling to cut down the thorns, adding nourishment to the soil, and offering safety and shade, so that eventually even the most withered fragile seedlings have a chance, over time, to grow into mature plants that will one day throw their seeds out into the world and create a harvest.

Dear Father, we are so sorry for the times when we have shirked the work you have allocated to us. Please can you give us another chance and help us find the courage to tackle whatever it might be. Amen

BRIDGET PLASS

Weeds in disguise

'The kingdom of heaven is like a man who sowed good seed… His enemy came and sowed weeds among the wheat… The servants asked him, "Do you want us to go and pull them up?" "No," he answered… "Let both grow together until the harvest."' (NIV)

Jesus didn't mince his words when it came to evil, and we are talking evil here: insidiously creeping under the surface, destroying innocence, attacking vulnerability, encouraging secrecy where depravity can flourish, strangling creativity, uglifying beauty.

Now I freely accept that some of the weeds that grow in my garden are not sown by anyone who cares about me! Especially, in my case, ground elder, which had taken pretty much total control of the garden before we moved in. It even managed to push its way through the tough membrane of our gravelled path.

Early attempts to deal with it meant pulling out quite a few of my newly planted tender seedlings before they could bloom. I grew to hate it and wished some angels would be despatched immediately to sort it out. But now I recognise the enemy. I know it by its leaves!

Jesus knew his farming audience. The tares he is speaking of (almost certainly darnel, a poisonous rye grass) were virtually undistinguishable, so, to prevent damaging the wheat, were best left until the harvest when they could be dealt with.

Jesus' warning is stark. Tares are good at disguise. Hidden killers, like coronavirus, are exactly that. Hidden. The tele-evangelist, the charismatic local leader, the recommended reading, the well-meant advice, even the people in your church are tares if they are affecting your spiritual growth negatively. And we are being told that God sees it all, that it makes him angry and that he will deal severely with it.

Dear Father, today we ask for wisdom to see the hidden threats to the growth of our faith and we ask for protection against hidden evil. Amen

BRIDGET PLASS

Yeast, alive or dead

He told them still another parable: 'The kingdom of heaven is like yeast that a woman took and mixed into about thirty kilograms of flour until it worked all through the dough.' (NIV)

This tiny parable has gained relevance for many of us. After years during which eating out was a regular part of our lives, the pandemic forced all of us back to our kitchens. Flour became a scarcity on supermarket shelves for months. Yeast was a much sought-after ingredient. Bread-making was turned into an art form. In fact, how best to create and then preserve your sourdough starter was discussed as avidly as any sports-related conversations of the past. So, too, was the fact that yeast can go bad when it is no longer active as a leavening agent in your bread.

Matthew records Jesus using this as a warning: 'Be on your guard against the yeast of the Pharisees and Sadducees' (Matthew 16:6), and Mark records Jesus saying: 'Watch for the yeast of the Pharisees and that of Herod' (Mark 8:15).

Yeast is an organism that lives and dies. A tiny amount of live good yeast can almost miraculously turn a pile of flour into a wonderful fragrant loaf. An equally tiny amount of bad dead yeast can, at best, produce a tough, smelly, hard lump and, at worse, create infection. How can we discern?

Bread-makers from the time of Jesus until now will tell us that all yeast may look the same but, when mixed with warm water, if your yeast is alive it produces wholesome-smelling bubbles and, when mixed into a dough and left for a while, the dough doubles in size. So, we are encouraged to test and sniff, and wait to see bubbles.

Dear Father, Jesus tells us he is the bread of life: fresh, wholesome, fragrant and essential for healthy growth. Today, we give thanks for the daily bread you offer us. Amen

BRIDGET PLASS

The hidden treasure and the pearl

'The kingdom of heaven is like treasure hidden in a field. When a man found it, he hid it again, and then in his joy went and sold all he had and bought that field… [It] is like a merchant looking for fine pearls. When he found one of great value, he went away and sold everything he had and bought it.' (NIV)

Do you know why I love these stories? It is because in both cases the men recognise they have found something beyond any normal expectation. And it is passion which causes them to do something quite crazy. You find a treasure, you bury the treasure, sell everything you have and buy the field. You find a pearl so exceptionally beautiful you sell everything to buy it. But here is a bit of a dilemma for us. What happened to all the 'counting the cost' stuff Jesus talks about elsewhere? Maybe they are one and the same.

We were in the township of Soweto, in South Africa, just after the famous election when Nelson Mandela became president. You can imagine the desperate poverty we encountered. Yet as we drove through the slum, we were astounded to see children walking to school in immaculately white socks and clean, albeit threadbare, uniforms. The daily effort that must have been involved to turn children out looking like that boggled our minds.

We saw it again in Zambia, where we met two orphan boys who walked nine kilometres to school every day on empty tummies. Education was a golden treasure, a pearl of great price, and whatever the personal cost they would grasp it.

Coming home, I reflected that education, being compulsory and often free, would probably not be described as pearls or treasure by most teenagers we knew! How easy for us to take for granted the priceless gift Jesus gave us on the cross and lose focus on its extraordinary value.

Paul knew all about cost and passion. In his letter to the Philippians he says, 'straining towards what is ahead, I press on towards the goal to win the prize for which God has called me heavenwards in Christ Jesus' (3:13–14).

Dear Father, help us to experience again the first joy of discovering the treasure that is your gift to us. Amen

BRIDGET PLASS

Equal pay

'A landowner… went out early in the morning to hire workers for his vineyard. He agreed to pay them a denarius for the day… About five in the afternoon he went out and found still others standing around… "You also go and work in my vineyard."' (NIV)

When my husband Adrian and I were in Africa to see the work being done by World Vision, we often saw men gathered at the side of dusty roads and were puzzled to see them still standing there when we returned much later in the day. What were they waiting for? We didn't know, but it occurred to us that maybe they were waiting to be picked for any work going. They were often excruciatingly thin, and many looked very poorly.

Early in the morning we had seen buses crammed with men being taken to places of work where presumably they would be paid, but what about these? If they had been picked up for work later in the morning, would they have received the same wage as the ones who had done a full day's work? Hard to believe. And what of those who were not chosen until late in the day or not at all? Would they eat that evening?

'Food security' is a phrase we have heard many times when travelling in the developing world: the difference between eating and not eating. The amazing thing about this story is that we are told our 'landowner' holds the view that everyone deserves rewarding equally, however frail, however beaten down, however useless they feel. And the glorious unfairness of this story represents everything good that Jesus wants us to know about his Father. Of course, he values and needs vigorous folk who can get up early in the morning and work their socks off, but he also values – and needs – the ones who have never really felt valued for anything; the frail in body, mind and spirit; in our world, the last picked. In God's kingdom they are up there with the best.

Dear Father, help us to see the world with your eyes, and please can you forgive us for the many times when we forget. Amen

BRIDGET PLASS

The lost son

'There was a man who had two sons. The younger one said to his father, "Father, give me my share of the estate"… [He] got together all he had, set off for a distant country and there squandered his wealth in wild living. After he had spent everything, there was a severe famine… He got up and went to his father.' (NIV)

The Germans call it home pain. We call it homesickness. The heart-wrenching yearning for a place where you felt safe and loved, especially when everything has gone wrong. I remember it. No prodigal, simply a restless, unhappy teenager longing to kick over the traces of my tidy upbringing. Careless of my parents' feelings, I set out for university eagerly anticipating a future crammed with adventure.

Lonely weeks later found me huddled sobbing in a phone box, frantically shoving in coins (yes, it was before mobiles) just to keep my mother's voice alive. She could have reminded me how selfish I'd been before leaving. She didn't. She received my pain and held on to me through that phone line until I was strong again.

The lost son knew he had squandered money and reputation, but had he also squandered the love of his father? Without the luxury of phoning home, the only way to find out was to face up, and for all of us this story sings of forgiveness, focusing on the wonderful, undeserved welcome home the prodigal received on his return.

Can we believe it for us? That no matter how or why we get lost, whether it's our fault or not, whether our motive for coming home is questionable, God yearns for us to experience homesickness, the overwhelming desire to return to the safety of his unconditional love. Throughout the Old Testament we hear the cry of the Father, 'Come home.' In Jeremiah he spells it out: 'You know the way home, it's the same way by which you left,' and he then goes on to say that he will light the way home, so you don't get lost again.

Dear Father, help us today to let the wonderful truth contained in this story penetrate the most despairing corners of our hearts. The truth is that the door is always open, and on the threshold stands love. Amen

BRIDGET PLASS

Let there be light...

Hannah Fytche writes:

Light. It surrounds us, illuminating worlds of colour, shape and movement. It is close to us, dancing on and around us, resting intimately with us. Without light, we would not be able to see. With light, we are awakened to a new vision of what is real and present.

Light glimmers throughout the Bible, from Genesis to Revelation. It sparkles when creation is described, appearing in literal depictions of the lights in the sky. More often, however, light, and its counterpart, darkness, are used metaphorically, to help us glimpse more of who God is, how he holds the world and who we are with him.

Throughout the next two weeks, we will journey with this imagery of light and darkness – both literal and metaphorical.

We will wonder at the shimmering advent of light – at creation and at Jesus' birth. We will delve into the depths with Job, confronting our questions about the darkness of suffering we experience in tension with the light of hope we hold on to. We will consider how the 'thick darkness' encompassing Mount Sinai's peak can be an image for God's presence, when we so often associate God's presence with light.

We'll see how Jesus opens eyes to the light of healing, hope, restoration – and the transformative knowledge of who he is. And we will be challenged to know our own identity as light, called to shine God's powerful, discerning and healing rays into the world.

My hope is that through this journey we will be brought close to God, for whom there is no darkness too dark. As the psalmist writes so stunningly, 'The night will shine like the day, for darkness is as light to you' (Psalm 139:12, NIV). I hope that we will be strengthened and encouraged by this knowledge, able to grow in our trust in God and our calling to shine with his light.

A prayer to begin: God, creator of lights, open our eyes to see the sparkle of your light. Give us the capacity to trust that you know and hold both light and darkness. Kindle in us the blazing fire of your love, that the way ahead may be illuminated by you. Amen

God speaks light

And God said, 'Let there be light,' and there was light. God saw that the light was good, and he separated the light from the darkness. God called the light 'day', and the darkness he called 'night'. (NIV)

As I write, I am sitting with my bare feet buried in soft grass and bathed in hot, spring sunlight. This is hard to imagine, perhaps, in November. It is hard to imagine, too, what it was like when God spoke and the very sun which is warming my toes came into existence.

Came into existence? Or spun? Erupted? Burst? Blew? Popped? Sparkled? Whispered into existence? My words cannot capture this moment of light's advent.

God's words, we read in Genesis, made the sun happen. Over the chaos of nothing at the start of it all, God's Spirit hovered and God's words are spoken. And light happens. The sun happens and later, as Genesis 1 relates, God also created the stars.

This is incredible. The poetry of Genesis 1 opens our hearts, if we let it, to God – God, whose huge imagination dreamt up beautiful, erupting light and whose words ordered and created it into being. Here in Genesis 1 we meet the God who has the first and last say, literally, over everything.

He has the first and last say over light and over dark. Over brightness and dimness. Over good and bad – although 'good' and 'bad', as we will see over the next two weeks, don't always map easily onto the metaphors of 'light' and 'dark'. Sometimes darkness is good. Sometimes light is hard. But we can know that God has the first and last words over it all.

At the start of these two weeks, therefore, spend some time becoming reacquainted with the God whose words made the sun happen. Let your imagination stretch wide: what was it like in that moment at the beginning of it all? Who is God, that his words can do such wonderful things?

Creator God, light happens because of your words. As I encounter the sun today and the stars tonight, may you place within me wonder at your power and creative imagination. May this move me to seek you more. Amen

HANNAH FYTCHE

Stars in the night

'Lift up your eyes and look to the heavens: who created all these? He who brings out the starry host one by one and calls forth each of them by name.' (NIV)

Yesterday we encountered the God whose words made light happen. Here we meet him again: he is the mighty one who brings out the starry host, one by one, into their place in the dark night's sky.

Eight and a half years ago, I was about to have an operation on my arm to remove some bone and translocate a nerve. A few nights before the operation, I was terrified. My dad took me on a walk to a coastal hillside, where marshland stretched below us and stars widened the sky above us. So many stars! Silver and sparkling, filling the dark expanse. A host of wonder.

As we watched the stars, I remembered Isaiah 40, and I was reassured. If God can bring out each of those myriad stars I could see before me, and if he knows each of them by name, surely he knows me by my name. Surely he could bring me out into the right place, even in the middle of a dark night, a scary situation. He has not disregarded me and he will not, just as he has not forgotten the stars.

In the following verse of Isaiah 40, God wonders why his people could think that he has disregarded them. 'Aren't the stars that you see evidence enough?' God asks them. 'Can't you see emblazoned even in the sky that I love you? I will not grow tired. I will not forget.'

With that, darkness becomes the backdrop for beauty. Fear turns to wonder at a God whose knowledge and love navigate dark nights and make them brilliant with stars.

He knows each light he's created by its name. He knows you by your name. You see, there is light and there is darkness. Together, coordinated by God, they are beautiful.

God, you know my name. When I face fear, remind me that you know me. Help me see the care with which you bring stars into place. Thank you for this light by which to navigate. Amen

HANNAH FYTCHE

Light speaks of God

The heavens declare the glory of God… They have no speech, they use no words; no sound is heard from them. Yet their voice goes out into all the earth, their words to the ends of the world. (NIV)

God speaks and light happens. And then: light speaks back. The heavens and all their lights declare God's glory, the psalmist writes. The lights of the sky proclaim the sheer wonder of their creator. By shining bright as they were made to do, the sky's lights communicate truth about the one who made them.

Light, from the perfectly distanced sun, heats the earth and nourishes all growing, living things. The creator of light must, therefore, have immense care for his creation, and immense precision to make these processes happen exactly as they are intended.

Light dazzles us with its exquisite beauty, melting the sky into gorgeous colours at sunrise and sunset. The creator of light must, therefore, have a great imagination and an incredible eye for beauty. Light tells us, in ways beyond words, how glorious the creator is.

I once saw a video in which Louie Giglio played recordings of stars – stars and the sounds they make. These sounds came from pulses of light and movement emanating from each star. They made intricate, eerily beautiful sound patterns.

Giglio layered individual stars' sounds on top of each other. Weaving together, they began to sound like a song. Finally, a recording of a worship song was added. (I think it was Chris Tomlin's 'How great is our God'.) It appeared as if the stars were joining in. They 'sung' worship! The stars give glory to God; the skies proclaim the work of his hands.

Light communicates to us the grandeur of our creator. We are invited to join in this proclamation – this pattern and song of worship – by the way in which we live our lives. If we live how we are created to live, we will shine bright. We will, with stars and sun and light and sky, tell the world of our God.

Creator God, the sky's lights shine with the truth of who you are. Thank you that you create with precision and adorn the world with beauty. Lead me into living in your design, that I too may illuminate the world. Amen

HANNAH FYTCHE

God knows light and darkness

'What is the way to the abode of light? And where does darkness reside? Can you take them to their places? Do you know the paths to their dwellings?' (NIV)

Job is one of my favourite books – which, if you are familiar with the story, might be surprising. Job's is a story of suffering, opening with the great darkness of his loss of family and livelihood. In his mourning, Job cries for his life to end. He calls for God to make 'gloom and utter darkness' claim the day of his birth, consigning him to the darkness of non-existence. It seems as if life has no light left for Job – no glimmering hope, no lamp to illuminate the way.

After extensive chapters of questions and grief, God's voice finally speaks. God answers from a whirlwind, a place of mystery, and opens Job's eyes to see anew.

Job saw utter, final darkness as the only outcome of his despair. God, however, questions this assumption by asking Job if he knows where light and darkness reside. 'Do you, Job, know the paths to their dwellings? Can you tell me how they work and what they mean? Are you great or know-ledgeable enough to know the answers?'

Job, of course, is not great or knowledgeable enough (as implied in 38:21). But God... *he* knows light's origin and he knows darkness's residence. Both light and darkness are known by God, held within his sovereignty.

God is saying: 'Although you don't know the answers, you can trust me to know them for you.'

Job can trust God because God knows light and darkness: no darkness is too dark for God.

This is why Job's story is one of my favourites: it doesn't give us answers, but it does show us that we can trust God even when light seems distant – and isn't this the glimmering hope we all need? Trust in God is the lamp that illuminates the way ahead.

Creator God, even when I cannot see or understand, you know all. You know the origins of light – and of darkness. Teach me to trust you even on dark or hard days. May my trust in you become my light. Amen

HANNAH FYTCHE

God revealed in thick darkness

When the people saw the thunder and lightning and heard the trumpet and saw the mountain in smoke, they trembled with fear... The people remained at a distance, while Moses approached the thick darkness where God was. (NIV)

Have you ever walked in high altitude as cloud or mist have descended around you? The closest I have been to this was on a walk in the Lake District, down a narrow, misty path bordered by auburn hillsides. I couldn't see five metres ahead and relied on the sight of my dad's red rucksack to show me the way!

In today's reading, God calls Moses to meet him on Mount Sinai. As Moses goes, the people remain distant, overwhelmed by the thunder and lightning, the trumpet sound and the smoke that announce God's presence. God thus appears to Moses in 'thick darkness'.

We could interpret this image as communicating God's unknowability, wrapping us up in an encounter with him that is beyond what our words can capture. As we saw yesterday, we are not as great or as knowledgeable as God: there is more to God than we could know or imagine. Darkness is a way of depicting this 'beyondness'.

But the 'thick darkness' of God is perhaps the bright brilliance of God, so bright that it becomes darkness – so bright that we cannot capture it with words or comprehend it with our minds. It is a dazzling darkness.

I imagine the Lake District once more. My dad's rucksack bobs out of view and I focus on the mystery of the mist and cloud around me. I have no words for what I see: it is beyond me. But this beyondness, this darkness, can be beautiful.

Remember when your experience of God has been beyond words – a feeling of presence, silent or unanswered prayer, or something else.

God, may I know you in the darkness of what I do not know, resting with trust in the unknowing. Amen

HANNAH FYTCHE

God revealed in darkness and brightness

He made darkness his covering, his canopy around him – the dark rain clouds of the sky. Out of the brightness of his presence clouds advanced, with hailstones and bolts of lightning… He reached down from on high and took hold of me; he drew me out of deep waters. (NIV)

In Psalm 18, God is described as accompanied by light and darkness. Hailstones and lightning attend him; smoke billows as he soars on wind's wings. Light and darkness flash around his movements. How often do you imagine God like this?

I would guess that the metaphors from the psalm's opening – rock, refuge, shield – are more familiar images. In our church songs, we sing about God being our shield and refuge, a safe and defended place in which we can find rest. Yet *both* images are used in Psalm 18: both are valid imaginings of and metaphors for God, revealing something of what he is like.

In that first image, then, God is depicted as so angry that he crackles with electricity and summons thunderous clouds to aid him. This reveals his powerful care for his people: so powerful that his anger (v. 7) at injury inflicted upon one of them (vv. 4–6) is poetised as a cosmic thunderstorm. God, wrapped in thunderous light and dazzling darkness, reaches down to draw the person for whom he cares out of the darkness of their suffering.

The psalmist later proclaims: 'You, Lord, keep my lamp burning; my God turns my darkness into light' (v. 28). God is so powerful that no darkness is too dark for him: he turns darkness into light (vv. 4–6). He sustains the psalmist's lamp – their glimmering hope, to illuminate the way ahead.

When we experience darkness, we can trust – like Job and the psalmist – that God, who knows the origins and workings of both light and darkness, can reach down from on high and take hold of us. Even though he doesn't give answers as to why we have experienced darkness, he reveals that he powerfully cares and will act with love for us.

Powerful God, although words cannot capture you, images can help us glimpse who you are. Thank you that you care for me. When I encounter darkness, may this image of your powerful love bring me light. Amen

HANNAH FYTCHE

Promised light

'Arise, shine, for your light has come, and the glory of the Lord rises upon you. See, darkness covers the earth and thick darkness is over the peoples, but the Lord rises upon you.' (NIV)

You might be familiar with these words from Epiphany, the day in January when we remember and celebrate the three kings' visit to Jesus. They speak of the joy that will come when God's light dawns over us, causing the darkness of the world to flee.

When Isaiah wrote these words, God's people lived in a difficult time and place. They were cast from their homes, waiting for God to rescue them. This waiting might have felt like a heavy, dark cloud pressing down on them. Not the thick darkness of Sinai that signified God's presence, but the thick darkness of oppression, loss and sin.

In the midst of this oppressive darkness, Isaiah points people towards the joy to come. 'Look,' Isaiah says, 'look, a light will come! There will be light shining into all the dark places – a light that will break darkness's heavy power. Glory will appear, and you will not have to wait for home any longer.'

When this light comes, people from afar will come with gifts to God's people: 'Nations will come to your light, and kings to the brightness of your dawn' (v. 3). They will come with gifts of gold and incense (remember the story of the Magi?), in what Isaiah imagines almost as a festival procession. The hearts of God's people will thrill and rejoice.

Isaiah's words are a promise of the joyful dawning – the advent – of Jesus. Jesus is the light that will arise upon the people, breaking the power of the world's darkness. Jesus is the light that reveals God to us: God, depicted as an unknowable, dazzling darkness, is here depicted as a light which we can know, a light which comes close to us to reveal God to us – as we will see in the next few days.

God of promise, centuries before Christ's dawning, you promised his arrival and the joy that it would bring. May I hold on to this promise today, and may joy grow in my heart over the wonderful light that you bring. Amen

HANNAH FYTCHE

Promise fulfilled

The light shines in the darkness, and the darkness has not overcome it. (NIV)

Here we see the promise fulfilled. The promise of the dawning of Christ's light becomes real and known, very present in the world.

It's about a month early, but imagine yourself in the nativity scene. Sit in the downstairs cave-stable of the inn and breathe in. Imagine the earthy, deep scent of the animals, and the smell even of Mary and Joseph after their long journey. All of a sudden, hear the bustle of a crowd of shepherds on the steps – and hear their hurry hush to wonder as they enter and see the tiny, newborn baby.

Tilt your ear to the ceiling as you catch the faint threads of angelic song from outside: 'Glory to God in the Highest! Peace to all people on earth! The light has dawned among us!'

Gaze at Mary in wonder and see in her eyes the awe that comes from holding the light of the world in her arms.

Hold on to this feeling of wonder: it is like the wonder of seeing the most glorious golden sunrise burst over the darkest horizon. It is the wonder of relief you feel across your shoulders when you let go of a long-held worry or fear. It is the wonder of seeing a terrible situation resolved into peace as you watch it unfold on the news.

It is the wonder of seeing goodness and wholeness spring up as God comes close to you in Christ Jesus, that tiny, newborn baby shining bright in the darkness of the cave.

Let that light shine into your whole day, your whole heart. Draw near to this Christ and let the light that he brings push back the dark and give you new joy, new life. This light shines in the darkness, and the darkness has not and will not ever overcome it.

Christ Jesus, you came to us as a baby so that you might draw close and show us who God is. Bring me to my knees in wonder. By this wonder, kindle in my heart the fire of your love. Amen

HANNAH FYTCHE

The life-light here with us

The true light that gives light to everyone was coming into the world. He was in the world, and though the world was made through him, the world did not recognise him. (NIV)

Have you ever been camping? You haul your heavy tent into a field and find a good pitch. You lay the tent on the ground and you thread poles into fabric loops. Suddenly the structure springs up and you hammer tent pegs into soft ground, holding ropes in place.

You stand back: here's home for the next few days, close to the earth.

In John 1:14, we read that the Word – Jesus, the light of the world – 'made his dwelling' among us. This phrase can also be translated 'pitched his tent'. Jesus pitched his tent among us; he created a temporary home in which to live and dwell close to the earth, close to his people.

The light of the world chose to be this close to the world he had made. He chose to live so intimately close to his creation – breathing the same air as us, eating the same food as us – that we might be made God's children. He shone with God's light at every turn: he taught forgiveness, love and grace; he healed wounds and societal rifts; he acted for justice and righteousness.

Jesus even shone with the light of God to the deepest darkness there is: death. And he rose again with the brilliance of light that overcomes every darkness. What a wonderful mystery: light to darkness to light; life to death to life.

Yet people did not and do not recognise him. The dazzling light of God is shining as close as is possible to them, as close as light is to their skin, and they do not see. We'll see more tomorrow of what it means for Jesus to open our eyes to light. But for now, let's dwell with the closeness of Christ. What does it mean to you that Jesus is close?

Jesus, you are light. May I know your closeness in my life as you desire for me to draw near. As I eat, work, sleep and breathe, may I know your presence, closer than light is to my skin. Amen

HANNAH FYTCHE

Life-light opening eyes

The blind man said, 'Rabbi, I want to see.' 'Go,' said Jesus, 'your faith has healed you.' Immediately he received his sight and followed Jesus along the road. (NIV)

This story glimmers with miraculous light, the light of healing and hope. Jesus makes a person with defective eyes see, and new freedom floods into Bartimaeus' life as daylight floods into his opened eyes.

Imagine what it felt like for Bartimaeus to see for the first time. There would have been awe as he began to identify the richness of colour; to gain a startling sense of perspective and movement; to see the strangeness and detail of people's faces; to match pictures with the sounds of his previously visionless world.

I understand this: my eyes struggle to see sometimes. My depth perception sometimes doesn't work, and blurriness is usual when I am stressed, tired or sensorially overwhelmed. It is an everyday miracle when my eyes work well with the light around me so that I can see, for example, a tree's branches reaching out in three sharp dimensions.

As well as the light of healing, this story glimmers with the light of new knowledge – the knowledge of who Jesus is. If we read this story within the structure of Mark's gospel, we notice that it has a partner in Mark 8, in which Jesus heals another blind man.

These stories bookend a section of Mark in which the disciples seek and discover who Jesus is. The sight given to them is sight of Jesus, and of the God who he came to earth to reveal. It is a vision that will ground them in Christ's love and shape them in Christ's life. Bartimaeus' words, 'Rabbi, I want to see,' become the prayer of all disciples: 'Rabbi, we want to see.'

Jesus our Rabbi, our teacher, open our eyes. Fill them with your new light of healing, hope and knowledge so that we can see and recognise you, the light among us.

Jesus, I want to see. I long for my eyes to be flooded with light of the knowledge of who you are, that my life may be grounded in your love and shaped by your life. Open my eyes, Rabbi. Amen

HANNAH FYTCHE

Brought out into the open

'For there is nothing hidden that will not be disclosed, and nothing concealed that will not be known or brought out into the open.' (NIV)

In Assisi in Italy, some friends and I bought a postcard for another friend. On the postcard was the dome of the Basilica di Santa Maria degli Angeli, which stands in the heart of the valley below Assisi. The dome was shrouded in mist; the image showed only the curve of the dome rising above white, obscuring cloud.

On the postcard's blank space, we wrote: 'There is nothing hidden that will not be disclosed, and nothing concealed that will not be known.'

We wrote it as an encouragement: there is nothing in the mystery of God that will not eventually be made known. There is nothing in the uncertainty and even darkness of this world that will not be brought out into the open and made clear. We can trust God to bring all things to light, just as the dome rises clear above the mist.

Bringing all things to light is what Jesus promises with these words. His discerning light will seek out every corner of the world, illuminating the secret places and the lost places. Light will show the way home from darkness. It will bring truth to the shadows of lies and deceit, and it will bring to justice every evil deed done under cover of night. We can trust God in this, knowing that his light is good.

We can partner with God, too, shining the gospel's discerning light into every place. God calls us to join him in illuminating the darkness and uncertainty of the world. It won't always be easy: shining the light of truth, justice and goodness into places of uncertainty, fear and destruction requires courage. But we are safe in the promise that there is no darkness that can overcome God's light. All will rise: there is nothing hidden that shall not be revealed.

God of justice, I trust that you will bring all things to light. I listen for places in this world into which you call me to shine. Give me wisdom and courage to go, shine and see your life arise. Amen

HANNAH FYTCHE

God's future revelation

From the throne came flashes of lightning, rumblings and peals of thunder. In front of the throne, seven lamps were blazing. These are the seven spirits of God. (NIV)

What a vision this is! Revelation 4 and 5 are stunning chapters of the Bible, overflowing with exquisite imagery of what God's throne room is like. There are gems, a rainbow, trumpet sounds. There is lightning flashing and thunder rumbling. It is mighty.

It is resonant of the imagery we glimpsed at Sinai and in Psalm 18: images of God wrapped in light and dark, crackling with electricity and power. This is God on the throne, overseeing the world's workings, worshipped by myriads of angels, blazing forth majesty's light.

When I picture this, I often have Jacqui Parkinson's tapestry of the 'Throne Room' in my mind. (It's from her series of tapestries entitled 'Threads through Revelation'; you can find this online.) The tapestry is filled with incredible colour, threads upon threads of bright purples, golds and blues. It is full of light, emanating from the throne which Jacqui depicts as an orb like the sun.

Later in Revelation, another vision is cast about God's new creation. In 21:23 we read: 'The city does not need the sun or the moon to shine on it, for the glory of God gives it light, and the Lamb [Jesus] is its lamp.' The sun, which God made happen, will no longer be needed: God's glory will be enough, shining forever and for all.

This is a promise that we can hold, as we live and wait in this world for the world to come. This is a promise that one day, we will be with God, entering his rest and being united with the one who calls us by name. It is a promise that, with the elders and angels around God's throne, we can join in the endless praise of God as we revel in the light of his glory.

Awesome God, thank you for visions of your majesty and new creation. Thank you for the glimpses they give of your power and wonder. May I hold on to the promise of your light, in which I will one day rest. Amen

HANNAH FYTCHE

Called to be light

'You are the light of the world. A town built on a hill cannot be hidden.'
(NIV)

You are light. You are created by the one who made the sun and the stars happen, the one who is enfolded in the dazzling darkness of everything we cannot know about him yet. Jesus has shown you this beyond-imagination, creator God: Jesus came to you as the light of the world to illuminate the way to the Father.

You know this light, and in his light you are made light. Shine.

Shine like the houses you see glittering from a distance in the dead of night, providing comfort for the traveller. Shine like the lighthouse perched on a clifftop, beaming light to guide ships safe to shore. Shine like the perfectly placed light of stars, whispering the promise of a God who knows each person by name. Shine to discern and to cut through darkness with truth and justice.

Shine: you are light.

The opening of today's reading gives some words that show us *how* to shine. Jesus says that they are blessed who are: poor in spirit, mourning, meek, hungering and thirsting for righteousness, merciful, pure in heart, striving for peace, persecuted for righteousness, rejoicing in God no matter what. Blessed are these people – they shine with God's blessing.

Consider which of these describes you today. Maybe you are acting on a burning hunger to see righteousness and justice in a situation. Because of this, you shine. Perhaps you are feeling low, poor in spirit and empty or hollowed-out. Yours is the kingdom of heaven, dear one. Because of this, Christ is here for you and you shine with his presence. Maybe you are pure in heart, working to choose the narrow gate and straight path rather than giving in to temptation. Because of this, you shine.

Whatever it is for you today, recognise and encourage it. This is how you shine.

Jesus, I shine because you are my light. May I recognise how I am shining your light. Can you help me to keep choosing to shine? I long to see your light illuminate our weary world. In your name, Amen

HANNAH FYTCHE

Even darkness is not dark

If I say, 'Surely the darkness will hide me and the light become night around me,' even the darkness will not be dark to you; the night will shine like the day, for darkness is as light to you. (NIV)

You know when you get words from songs stuck in your mind, humming insistently through your day? I sometimes get that with these words – not to a tune, just to the rhythm of their poetry and promise: 'Even the darkness will not be dark to you, the night will shine like the day, for darkness is as light to you. Even the darkness will not be dark.'

So on it goes.

On it always goes: the darkness will never be dark to God because he knows the origins of both light and darkness. Even more: darkness will shine like the day; all that is hidden will be made known by the all-seeing, deeply discerning, dazzling light of God.

This is a promise, always there and never stopping. No darkness is too dark for God. The night will shine like the day. Darkness is as light to him.

I am so comforted by this promise. There is nowhere I can go that will be too dark for God's light to reach me. There is no darkness that our world can fall into that is too dark for his rescue – no tears too bitter, no destruction too final. There is always the powerfully glimmering hope of God's light, ready and eager to illuminate and bring new life.

I wonder: what is in your heart that you need to entrust to this promise today? Is it worry? Is it grief? Is it fear for our world? What weighs on you, dear heart?

As you remember this weight or this darkness, let God bring his light to it. Even this darkness is not dark to him; this night will shine like the day because darkness is as light to him. And with him close to you, you will shine.

Father God, be gentle with my sense of darkness. But always bring your light too, reminding me that there is no darkness too dark for you. Your light will always find me, and you will always bring new life. Amen

HANNAH FYTCHE

Mary's song of praise

Anne Le Tissier writes:

It is that time of year when some of us may consider making New Year's resolutions, while others may have been put off from previous failed attempts. But any resolution at any time of year requires resolve to fulfil it. To lose weight, study the Bible, learn a new skill or invest more time in a relationship, we need to be fixed in our purpose and intention, determined to commit no matter what else may try to lure us away. And our determination will strengthen the more we long for or care about the thing we want to achieve.

Whatever goals we may have for 2022, the Westminster Catechism suggests a resolution that should top all of our lists: 'Man's chief end is to glorify God, and to enjoy him forever.' This 'chief end' or 'primary purpose' to glorify God is the theme undergirding the Magnificat; a word that means 'glorifies', and the name given to Mary's outpouring of prophetic praise and proclamation in response to conceiving God's child (Luke 1:46–55).

'My soul glorifies the Lord and my spirit rejoices in God my Saviour,' she begins (NIV). It is one thing to sing *about* God's glory, but *to* glorify him as Mary did is to live in such a way that we reveal and reflect the love, beauty, holiness, forgiveness, faithfulness, grace, mercy, wisdom, provision, equipping, empowering… that God first lavished on us.

And that doesn't happen passively because we believe in God; it needs resolve – a committed intention – to pursue it; for the tense of 'glorifies' is not a one-off action but ongoing. To glorify God requires consistency to follow through, and Mary reveals both the 'why' and the 'how' we might do that, through the rest of her song.

Even as I begin writing, I am challenged about my resolve to glorify God, rather than my personal goals, unhelpful cravings or ungodly attitudes. My flesh is weak, but scripture is rich with truth and promises that inspire and strengthen the resolve I need. The question is, do I only believe them in my head, or also in my soul and spirit – in the entirety of my being, as Mary did? Join me this week, as Mary suggests how our lives, and not just our words, may become a Magnificat in themselves – glorifying God in every way.

God sees you

'My soul glorifies the Lord and my spirit rejoices in God my Saviour, for he has been mindful of the humble state of his servant.' (NIV)

Many years ago, I suffered a prolonged period of feeling spiritually dry. I felt barely able to pray but clung to one verse in desperate faith. No one knew, not even my husband, so imagine my astonishment when I received a handmade card in the post, displaying that very verse! God had seen me, he was mindful of my situation, and his loving care and purpose were restored to my heart.

Hagar also encountered the God who saw her (Genesis 16:1–16). Despite her abusive situation, God counselled her, encouraged her and gave promises for her future. And although Mary's situation was so different to Hagar's, she too was deeply moved after receiving the news that proved God had been 'mindful' of her (see also Luke 1:26–38).

I relish that word, 'mindful'. It means to notice, to pay attention or respect to, to look favourably on. It is more than an awareness of someone, it is an extended knowledge, care and appreciation of them.

The 'humble state' of Mary's life suggests she was relatively unknown except to her family and community; she had no gifting or responsibility that would mark her out in a crowd. But the awesome realisation dawned that, despite her humble state, Israel's almighty divine Sovereign had seen her and knew her among thousands of Israelites, including hundreds of scribes and priests; a woman in a male-dominated culture from the disdained town of Nazareth. No wonder her adoration and delight flowed so freely and sincerely.

Whether your life and circumstances are traumatic or routine, admired or ignored, upfront or behind the scenes, successful in the world's eyes or struggling, God is mindful of you, too. Receive that truth today, letting it comfort and reassure you deep within your being, and inspire your own delight in his loving care.

I don't know your circumstances, but I do know this from God's word: God sees you. He cares for you. He values you. He wants to work through you. How does that encourage you? Respond to him now in prayer.

ANNE LE TISSIER

Yield to God's will

Continue to work out your salvation with fear and trembling, for it is God who works in you to will and to act in order to fulfil his good purpose. (NIV)

What comes to mind when you read 'servant'? It's not a particularly pleasant concept. And yet, this is how Mary described herself in Luke 1:38 and 48, often translated as 'slave-woman' or 'handmaiden'.

Mary, however, described herself as God's 'servant' for positive reasons, for unlike forced servitude, she did not serve a harsh taskmaster. She knew the God of her ancestors for his justice, mercy, provision, righteousness, loving kindness and faithfulness. So devoted was her response to her deeply rooted belief that she did not need to be coerced into serving him; she willingly obeyed without hesitation and with no thought of reward, despite knowing it could cost her dearly with divorce, shame, estrangement or even death by stoning.

To live the life of Magnificat is to glorify God through willing obedience to his word and by yielding to his will. So let's consider what might be holding us back from saying 'yes', without hesitation or fear, to the prompting of God's word and Spirit to our hearts. Personally, I'm being encouraged to forgo certain comforts which distract me from seeking him with *all* my heart, that in turn I may know the fullness of his presence working through me.

In the past, I've held back through fear of failure, feelings of inadequacy and worries over what people would think. There have even been times I've said 'no' to God because I did not fully trust him for material provision. What about you? Can you say with heartfelt sincerity, 'I am the Lord's servant'? Identify specifically what might be holding back your 'yes' to his promise of life to the full in Jesus (John 10:10), then talk to him about it in prayer.

To live the life of Magnificat is to obey God's word and yield to his will, not to earn his favour or appease his anger, but to encounter him as our source, resource, equipping and enabling of true life.

ANNE LE TISSIER

Would others call me blessed?

'Cursed is the one who trusts in man... But blessed is the one who trusts in the Lord, whose confidence is in him.' (NIV)

I have worked from home for many years, but during last year's pandemic lockdown, I developed new rhythms to my day. One was to pause with my afternoon cuppa to read a psalm instead of working through, then give space for God to inspire me in prayer for my neighbours. I had been praying for them at least weekly for years, but the pandemic inspired the formation of a neighbourhood WhatsApp group, increasing our connection and, in turn, becoming a prompt for daily prayer.

The more I prayed, however, the more I questioned how much of Jesus they encountered in me. Did they perceive me as contented or striving, calm or anxious, critical or positive, secure or fearful, gentle or assertive, considerate or domineering, compassionate or insensitive, selfless or controlling, gracious or judgemental? In short, would they describe me as 'blessed', as someone with an assured perspective on life that they would desire for themselves?

Mary's rapturous Magnificat proved God's presence and purpose were the source of her blessing, not her possessions or circumstances. Mary was insignificant to the world at that time, but the 'Mighty One' who was at work in her life would, in turn, work mightily in the world so that others would call her blessed (Luke 1:48b–49).

God has done great things for us, too. In giving us life in Jesus we have access to heavenly blessings which enrich and empower us. We are blessed with assurance, peace, poise, contentment, equipping, guidance, significance and strength of well-being, as we remain open and receptive to his word and Spirit. No matter the difficulties we face or what we may long for this Christmas, let's determine to put our trust in God when tempted to succumb to wavering emotions of doubt, fear, defeat, discouragement, selfishness or negativity.

Lord, I yearn that my life would be fruitful and influential for you. I choose today to put my confidence in your presence and promises; I open my heart to steady my emotions with your truth. Amen

ANNE LE TISSIER

Love-inspired reverence

'Do not lay a hand on the boy,' [God] said. 'Do not do anything to him. Now I know that you fear God, because you have not withheld from me your son, your only son.' (NIV)

After many years living in rented and then church accommodation, my husband and I were delighted with God's guidance and provision to buy a home. I loved it from the first viewing, a love that grew over the years, distracting my time, focus, energy and resources from seeking first God's greater kingdom purposes for my life. A day came, however, when I sensed God's conviction that I was loving his gift more than the giver.

'Love' is a word I repeatedly use while singing worship songs or praying, but Mary doesn't use the word 'love' in her outpouring of devotion and proclamation of praise; she uses the word 'fear' (Luke 1:50). To fear the Lord is to love and delight in God more than anyone or anything else. It is to worship – to love, adore, honour, respect and revere – the essence and nature of God's character, purposes, promises and power, more than our own feelings, reactions, opinions or dreams.

Abraham's willingness to obey God in sacrificing his treasured son is a stark reminder of this. Loving, fearing and obeying God are intrinsic to each other (1 John 5:3). To fear God, that is, to fear defiling his character with our attitudes and behaviour, or fear wasting our life pursuing selfish wants and priorities instead of God's kingdom, is paramount to living the life of Magnificat – to glorifying God.

But, as Mary reminds us, it is also a life assured and comforted by his mercy, his compassion and loving kindness extended to all who revere him as Lord. The alternative is to worship idols; anything or anyone we depend on, delight in or pursue more than God.

Who or what commands the loving allegiance of your heart?

Lord, I name the idols which distract my devotion and resources or undermine your holy presence. Grow in me a fear of missing out on your offer of life to its full potential, to guard me against their undermining influence. Amen
ANNE LE TISSIER

Resetting our values and priorities

His disciples came to him, and he began to teach them. He said:
'Blessed are the poor in spirit, for theirs is the kingdom of heaven.'
(NIV)

To reset a mobile phone to its original factory settings erases all the apps and data since its purchase, restoring the equipment to its original created design. But it is not just technological inventions that get changed by the user. God created us in his image, but his kingdom values, perspective and priorities have been tampered with and, at times, changed beyond recognition through our fallen, sinful nature and wills.

This metaphorical image of a reset button helps us understand Mary's prophetic assurance of what Jesus would accomplish in the world, as if it had already happened (Luke 1:51–53). Mary describes how God turns human attitudes, values and class structures upside down, a prophecy repeatedly affirmed throughout scripture, not least through Jesus' own life and teaching.

This broad brushstroke of truth for the world's standards and priorities is also pertinent to us. We are called to live out God's kingdom values whatever our circumstances. Where the world esteems benchmarks of success defined by cultural ideals and expectations, God defines success as a life yielded to his character and commands, bearing the 'fruit' of his presence. Where the world shapes a sense of identity, significance or worth from certain roles or responsibilities, we are called to be moulded and motivated, freed and fulfilled by our identity as God's child, and the way *he* chooses to work through us.

As we seek to live the life of Magnificat which glorifies God, this passage prompts some questions: whose values am I living out or trying to live up to? Whose perspective informs, inspires, steers, shapes and drives my focus and goals? Do I need to press the reset button in any area of my life, to restore it to my creator's original intentions?

Lord, you look at the heart. Forgive me when I focus on my own or others' outward appearance. Purify my heart of self-motivated goals, refine my values with your holy ways and reset my goals with your priorities. Amen

ANNE LE TISSIER

Magnificat prayer

God exalted him to the highest place… that at the name of Jesus every knee should bow, in heaven and on earth and under the earth, and every tongue acknowledge that Jesus Christ is Lord, to the glory of God the Father. (NIV)

Alongside our own prime minister, I have been burdened for many years to pray for the presidents of Eritrea and North Korea. I won't pretend I don't feel discouraged at times. Reports of Christian persecution and impoverishment at the hands of these governments cause me to question if God is hearing my prayers and why, after so many years praying with thousands of others, these – and indeed, many other violent or dictatorship regimes – continue to rule, seemingly undeterred. But my discouragement soon wanes as I hear repeated stories of God moving in the lives of his people in these countries. My faith, too, is reassured when I recall the truth of our reading, that every knee, including those of unbelieving kings, presidents and prime ministers, will one day bow to King Jesus.

'He has brought down rulers from their thrones,' Mary proclaimed and prophesied (Luke 1:52). I may not see God's influence that the world's rulers are resisting, but I can believe with utmost certainty that one day they will kneel before Jesus. My role is not to give in to discouragement but to persevere in prayer, filled with God's compassion and mercy for the desperate need of these leaders to choose to submit to their saving Lord, before they find themselves forced to when they meet him face to face. For God wants *all* people, including 'kings and all those in authority… to come to a knowledge of the truth' (1 Timothy 2:2, 4).

Is there a particular world leader who you find yourself thinking about more than most? Perhaps God is calling you to commit this coming year to be in prayer for the eyes of their heart to be opened to his saving grace; that they in turn may glorify him, too.

'Bring to an end the violence of the wicked and make the righteous secure – you, the righteous God who probes minds and hearts' (Psalm 7:9). Amen
ANNE LE TISSIER

Blessed to be a blessing

'He has helped his servant Israel, remembering to be merciful to Abraham and his descendants forever, just as he promised our ancestors.' (NIV)

I can clearly recall the day God answered my prayers while at a YWAM conference, saying: 'Freely you have received; freely give' (Matthew 10:8). I was seeking which mission trip to be part of, and while my spirit was drawn to India, my head and heart were hesitant owing to additional costs required, the meagre accommodation and the sickness we'd likely suffer. But God was calling me to bless others with the blessings he had given me, even if it used up my savings. Even if it would call upon every reserve of grace, patience, energy, wisdom, discernment and courage; just some of the blessings I would need to receive from him daily, to then share with others.

Despite personal cost, Mary accepted God's purpose without hesitation, delighting in how he would continue to fulfil his promise to bless 'all nations' (Genesis 22:16–18). Her joy was not limited to what God had done *for* her, but for what God would do for others *through* her. God reminds me of this regularly. He has blessed me with a home that I may freely share it with others in need of hospitality. He has blessed me with chickens and a vegetable garden to share, not hoard, the fruit of my pleasure-filled labours. He has blessed me with his gift of teaching, that he may bless others through me no matter how nervous or inadequate I feel.

What we have may appear simple or insignificant compared to mothering the Messiah, but every gift of God received and shared has the power to influence someone's despair with hope, cynicism with faith, need with provision, and their experience of the problematic world with the light and truth of God's kingdom power. I trust such fruit will inspire our own delight in God, too.

'My soul glorifies the Lord, and my spirit rejoices in God my Saviour.' Lord, may this truth be my living reality, throughout and beyond the Christmas period, for your presence is truly my very best gift. Amen

ANNE LE TISSIER

Tender comfort
(Elizabeth and Zechariah)

Fiona Barnard writes:

'God loves you and has a wonderful plan for your life.' That is what they say. The truth of it bestows us a purpose and a hope. Yet sometimes we struggle to visualise it amid dirty socks, troublesome colleagues, trashed plans and too-many-things-to-do-before-Christmas panic.

The glorious promises of scripture can, in turns, be heartening and hollow, ambiguous and astounding, and often, we may conclude, meant for someone else. Many times they work out in ways we do not expect. Yet if we look closely, we see the hand of a tender God whose Great Big Story is populated with myriads of simple, beautiful stories of surprised men and women, individuals who find themselves swept up into his promises, families who will only understand in eternity the marvel of his sovereign plans.

In Advent, we often hear these verses: 'Comfort, comfort my people *with gentle, compassionate words*. Speak *tenderly* from the heart… A *thunderous* voice cries out in the wilderness: "Prepare the way *for* Yahweh's arrival!… Yahweh's radiant glory will be unveiled"' (Isaiah 40:1–5, TPT).

And so it will. Soon. But before that, before we listen to the thunderous voice crying in the wilderness, we overhear the cries of a childless couple. Before God's dazzling glory is revealed, we see great sorrow alongside faithfulness. Before heaven comes to earth to fulfil God's saving purposes for the nations, we meet a husband and wife just going about the business of Jewish ritual and prayer. It happens here: tender, earth-shattering comfort finds a home, a space in the disappointment and hopes of an ordinary couple just getting on with life in the Judean hill country.

As we travel this Advent, our sorry world may seem like the last place where 'Yahweh's radiant glory will be unveiled'. Perhaps we think that our daily grind is so watertight and prescribed that tender comfort and new life have no chance of seeping in. We may imagine wistfully that this is someone else's story for another time. But listen. Listen to that distant cry, the voice first heard in the wilderness. The song born of surprise. The lyrics crafted in love. The chorus which gathers up God's community into one. Listen. It calls to you.

Getting to know them

There was a Jewish priest named Zechariah who served in the temple... His wife, Elizabeth, was also from a family of priests... They were both lovers of God, living virtuously and following the commandments of the Lord fully. But they were childless since Elizabeth was barren, and now they both were quite old. (TPT)

'This is Eric and he looks at the sun.' I considered my words a good enough introduction to a lecture by a world-famous solar physicist. Brief maybe, but sufficient! My husband's startled reaction took me grovelling to the Most Esteemed Professor who was also a Master of Gracious Forgiveness. It was a lesson in the finer points of résumé elaboration. How *do* you sum people up?

Luke does it pretty well here. In a few words, he answers the questions we generally ask, aloud or privately: Where are you from? What do you do? What is important to you? What are you like? How about your family?

Meet Zechariah and Elizabeth, our companions this week! They live in the hill country of Judea during tense political times. In Jewish eyes, Zechariah and Elizabeth are highly honoured because both are from priestly families. Later in the gospels, we hear negative things about the religious rulers, but this couple are faithful through and through.

They don't just say correct words and perform rituals efficiently. They live out their calling 24/7. They love the Lord with heart, soul, mind and strength. However, there is a 'but'. Their devotion has not secured them the promised Old Testament blessing of family. In a culture where this brings shame, Elizabeth bears painful stigma because she cannot bear a child.

How do you introduce yourself? What do you love and prioritise? How about the 'but' you rarely reveal: the emptiness, disappointment, shame? God had not spoken to his people for 400 years since the prophet Malachi promised a new Elijah to announce the Lord's coming. Perhaps God's silence towards you feels almost as long. Yet you continue to love him. Keep holding on faithfully. He may yet surprise you.

Zechariah's name means 'The Lord has remembered'. What do you long for the Lord to remember about you?

FIONA BARNARD

The smell of surprise

A large crowd of worshippers had gathered to pray outside the temple at the hour when incense was being offered. All at once an angel of the Lord appeared to [Zechariah], standing just to the right of the altar of incense. Zechariah was startled and overwhelmed with fear. (TPT)

Smells help you remember. The sweet scent of the rose next to me, gifted when my mother died, reminds me of her. Just now when I opened my father's book, I inhaled a whiff of his study. It catches you unawares. It can burst open those film clips in your store of memory and emotion.

Twice a year, Zechariah exchanges the smells of rural Judea for the many odours of downtown Jerusalem. He takes his turn to serve in the temple he knows well. Many times he has stood outside with the crowd for the twice daily burning of incense. Today, however, is a once-in-a-lifetime moment for him. He has been chosen to enter the holy place and offer the worship of God's people.

In this sacred space, the fragrance of prayer is so much stronger, overwhelming his mind and heart. The aroma reminds him of that priestly privilege across the centuries, where God invites his people to adore him through a representative. The oil expresses their desire for a deliverer and their cries for forgiveness. Perhaps unbidden, his own heartfelt longing for a son is triggered by the perfume of prayer. The years of dashed hopes mingle with the aroma of holy awe. Suddenly, without warning, an angel interrupts his prayerful meditation. Most unexpected.

On a church day away, I caught the whiff of a familiar lavender and rosemary oil, which took me back several years. I had used it for months to massage surgery scars. 'Lord, please heal!' I'd prayed. Struggling to face the wounds, I had redirected my prayers to healing my deeply broken church community. But I didn't think it possible. Now, as I surveyed the smiles amid prayer and discussion, I was overwhelmed with joy: God had actually heard my prayer.

Today, as you come to pray, you don't need to wait outside a temple: you can go right into the presence of God. Why not light a sweet-smelling candle to help you focus? Lay your life, love and intercession before him.

FIONA BARNARD

Butterfly wings

'Your prayer for a child been answered. Your wife, Elizabeth, will bear you a son… He will be filled with the Holy Spirit… He will persuade many … to turn back to the Lord… He will prepare a *united people* who are ready for the Lord's appearing.' (TPT)

You add one more apple to the fruit bowl, one more coat to the wobbly peg, one more brick to the Jenga tower – and it all comes crashing down! That is my domestic version of the chaos theory: when a butterfly flaps its wings in the Amazonian jungle, a storm causes havoc in Europe. It is the tiny things that really change the world.

In the Jerusalem temple, a lone priest performs the ritual of prayer on behalf of the people. It has been done twice a day for as long as anyone can remember. But on this day, an angel shows up. At this hour, the Lord speaks. At this moment, God's answer comes tumbling down through years of agonised petition. Decades of prayer: waiting and wondering, wearied and watchful, are stored in the vaults of God's gracious promises. Until today, like a snowball growing as it rolls, it gathers up every plea for deliverance, every appeal for a messianic Saviour, every longing for forgiveness and reconciliation. Beautifully, it also collects one couple's now impossible hope for a baby. Today as Zechariah holds up the incense-filled prayers in arms of surrender, God cries out, 'Yes, yes, yes!'

The time has come. This child will not only bring delight to his parents, but will also be great in God's sight, going 'before the Lord as a forerunner, with the same power and anointing as Elijah the prophet'. In the sovereignty of God, the answer to the intimate prayers of Elizabeth and Zechariah is wrapped up in the panoramic designs for the coming of God himself to heal a troubled nation. The flapping butterfly wings of a faithful, childless couple are going to shake a broken world to behold the splendour of their God: the one who has held every single prayer close to his heart.

Dare I trust that the desires God places on my heart might be part of a much greater, more exciting plan to work out his saving purposes? Oh Lord, count me in to what you are doing!

FIONA BARNARD

Beyond words

'He has sent me to announce to you this good news. But now, since you did not believe my words, you will be stricken silent and unable to speak until the day my words have been fulfilled at their appointed time and a child is born to you. That will be your sign!' (TPT)

'Did Tracy enjoy her 40th birthday celebrations?' I asked her husband. A flash of pain tore across his almost smiling face: 'Yes, we went to a show, had a meal…' But it was what he *didn't* say that I think I heard speaking even louder: 'She was miserable. We both were. Forty feels too old to have a baby. It is another landmark in the loss of hope.' Sometimes the most monumental cares of our lives are the least expressed aloud, for our protection.

In the hushed sanctuary, Zechariah's disappointed hopes of being a father are exposed as stoical resignation. It may be too painful to talk about any more, but in the privacy of that conversation with God's messenger, he swipes back at the promise as though it were a mocking insect: 'How do you expect me to believe this? I'm an old man and my wife is too old to give me a child. What sign can you give me to prove this will happen?' ('I am weary of false optimism.')

The sign he receives is puzzling: he becomes mute. When he emerges, shaken and gesturing to the waiting crowd, he cannot perform the expected ritual blessing. This priest has nothing to offer a prayerful crowd. For in a most sacred moment, he dared not believe in a God who reverses human biology and intervenes in history. He continues his service in the temple with nothing to say.

He goes home, unable to explain what has happened. For months, at least nine, he must play a game of charades with Elizabeth and his incredulous local community. In the absence of speaking, he has time to ponder the puzzling ways of God as his post-menopausal wife grows big with his baby. The faith of barren Elizabeth and mute Zechariah expands and bursts forth in joyful praise.

'See how kind it is of God to gaze upon me,' says Elizabeth. How is God gazing on you amid the unutterable disappointments or unexpected surprises of your days?

FIONA BARNARD

Be with me!

Mary arose and hurried off… to the village where Zechariah and Elizabeth lived. Arriving at their home, Mary entered the house and greeted Elizabeth. At the moment she heard Mary's voice, the baby within Elizabeth's womb jumped and kicked. And suddenly, Elizabeth was filled to overflowing with the Holy Spirit! (TPT)

'You'll never believe what's just happened!' When I say these words to you, your reaction is hugely important. Please don't fail to look up or listen half-heartedly or point out that what's just happened is unremarkable or unreal. Plenty of others will do that. My spirit will nosedive.

As Elizabeth's stomach swells with the child inside her, there must be so many questions which neither she nor the dumbfounded Zechariah can answer. Guarding her precious charge, secluded from the village tittle-tattle, she waits. One day, she hears the voice of her teenage cousin Mary at the door, and suddenly her whole being is awash with God's Spirit and the baby within her leaps in sheer delight.

Together, like a two-part, unpractised yet beautiful harmony, these women experience a profound knowingness, a joy which floods them both. Recognition, confirmation, wonderment and new understanding captivate them as they embrace. 'I do believe what's happened! Thousands won't, but I do! Mary, you are favoured. You believed what the Lord said. The child within you will bring God great delight. He will change everything!'

And over the next three months, they unravel the questions and implications of it all, anxiety accompanying awe. Both are bound together with a remarkable, spine-tingling sense that the almighty God of history is on the move, and they are part of the action.

So when the Lord touches my life, be Elizabeth to me! Accompany me in the wisdom and joy of the Holy Spirit. Tell me you are all ears, enter my story, join me in the emotion of my tale, give me the space I need to explore the impact of what I relate. You will bless me beyond measure. And you too will be blessed.

Lord God, give me a listening heart in my encounters today. Amen

FIONA BARNARD

The Lord is gracious

When the baby was eight days old, according to their custom, all the family and friends came together for the circumcision ceremony. Everyone was convinced that the parents would name the baby Zechariah, after his father. But Elizabeth spoke up and said, 'No, he has to be named John!' (TPT)

'Same old, same old': I quite like that expression. It tickles me because it is usually uttered with a roll of the eyes, a feigned boredom. Sometimes traditional ways have a finite shelf life, despite all their comforting familiarity.

As friends and family gather to celebrate the miracle son in the customary circumcision ceremony, they get a surprise. 'Different new, different new' rings out as the baby is named. This message delivered by the angel to Zechariah is now embodied these nine months later in this child. No, he is not going to be given the family name, though he has a godly heritage. He is to be called a brand-new name: John, meaning 'the Lord is gracious'.

The astonished onlookers forget Zechariah is mute, not deaf, and make signs to confirm his wife's decision! But as he writes 'His name is John', his voice is released, and his praise resounds over his son's cries: 'God *is* gracious!' He has always been gracious, but this is a harbinger of a 'different new' as he is on the move, graciously preparing a people for Jesus' coming. In fact, this naming ceremony combines the 'same old' of Jewish covenantal faithfulness with the promise of 'different new', as this noisy surprise points forward to a Saviour, the hope of the world.

God is gracious. As you look back over this past year and come closer to celebrate the birth of Jesus, how have you seen the gracious hand of God in your life and in that of your community? In the waiting and the wonder, the disappointments and the delights, the answered prayers and the unexpected encounters, how have you witnessed his goodness? Can you trust him for the 'different new' the coming year will bring?

Gracious God, as past and future merge especially poignantly at this time of year, I cling to your goodness and mercy. Amen

FIONA BARNARD

Soon, now and not yet

'The splendour light of heaven's glorious sunrise is about to break upon us in holy visitation, all because the merciful heart of our God is so very tender. The word from heaven will come to us with dazzling light… He will illuminate the path that leads to the way of peace.' (TPT)

As we inch closer to Christmas, amid the many calls of the present, it seems we also straddle past and future. Great aunt's seasonal recipes renew their mandatory call to be included in the festive menu; cards from friends containing the year's catch-up take us back to 'the old days'; we judder like slightly deranged robots to relive traditions. Simultaneously, the diary for 2022 is already filling up, though since the Covid-19 pandemic we are perhaps less sure of what we might write in pen rather than pencil.

Prophets, too, seem to get their past, present and future all muddled up. As Zechariah bursts into praise, he recalls God's ancient promises to Abraham, King David and the prophets: promises of freedom and salvation, forgiveness and peace. In John's birth they shine now like the first rays of dawn after nights dominated by enemy hatred and despair.

So sure is he of God's liberation that he speaks of this future as though it has happened already. His vision extends way beyond his baby's childhood. This God, who has touched his life profoundly, has shown mercy to all. He has already rescued them. Poignantly, he sees his own priestly role as redundant: 'Now we can boldly worship God with holy lives,' he declares, 'living in purity as priests in his presence every day!'

All these centuries later, we may lament, 'But this world is still so dark. Oppression and bondage, poverty and misery blight the lives of many, including your people. What happened?' This Advent, we pray to share Zechariah's faith-filled eyes to see afresh how Jesus' coming ushered future hope into the present. We crave a godly faithfulness like his to enter prayerfully and practically into the ongoing working out of Christ's salvation. We cry anew, 'Come, Lord Jesus!'

'Praise be to the exalted Lord God of Israel, for he has seen us through eyes of grace, and he comes as our Hero-God to set us free! He appears to us as a mighty Saviour, a trumpet of redemption' (vv. 68–69).

FIONA BARNARD

God's promises to those who wait

Sheila Jacobs writes:

Waiting! During the coronavirus pandemic, I (like everyone else) felt as if 'waiting' had become part of my daily life. Waiting patiently in a queue. Being patient about what was available and what wasn't when we bought our weekly groceries. Waiting for goods to be delivered or for things to be repaired, or for phone calls to be answered.

I don't like waiting. I generally live life at around a million miles per hour. If something goes wrong in the house or with the car, I try to get it fixed immediately. I'm not into procrastination. Waiting just doesn't come naturally to me.

The nation of Israel had a very long wait until God spoke to them in the person of his Son. The gap between the Old and New Testaments was around 400 years. God's people often find there is a waiting period for God to speak or to act. Clearly divine time isn't our time. God never seems to be in a hurry. He isn't frantic. He isn't just peaceful – he *is* peace.

Waiting for the birth of the Saviour, then, meant not hours, days, months or even years, but centuries. At this very special time of year, we're waiting too. But it isn't a wait that feels frustrating. It is a wait of anticipation. God is about to do something new. There are promises that can only be fulfilled in the time of waiting – even though God never promises those times will be easy.

In uncertain times, it's comforting to think about how we can connect with the one who knows the future and who has a plan. His plan was to send his Son to save us from the consequences of our sin; our turning away from him. That was the first Advent. And now we await the second Advent, when Jesus will come again.

We don't know when that will be, but we can look forward in anticipation. Just as in the first Advent when people saw him face to face, so we too will one day see him. Until that time, we have the opportunity to discover the treasures of waiting. So come with me on a journey of waiting, of finding God's promises in the stillness and the delight that come from rest.

Just wait!

Moses answered them, 'Wait until I find out what the Lord commands concerning you.' Then the Lord said to Moses… (NIV)

The story of Moses is an intriguing one: it's a story of a man trying to serve God in his own strength, but then, in weakness, finding himself commissioned!

In this passage we see his wisdom in dealing with an important issue concerning the people he was leading. He wasn't jumping in with an answer. He wasn't guessing what the Lord might want them to do. He was telling them to *wait* until he found out what God's view was on the matter.

So often we make important (and not so important) decisions without really consulting God. We may shoot up a prayer and hope for the best, but don't really wait to see what God might say. Sometimes we have to make snap judgements. But generally, we find we can – if we want to – spend time waiting for God to speak. It depends on how much we want to know his heart.

At this time of year, it's so easy to fall into the trap of 'hurry'. We feel stressed and pressurised to produce the perfect Christmas. There are things to buy, presents to wrap, people to see. But what about the one whom we are celebrating? Are we so busy with 'stuff' that we forget to spend time with him, asking how he would like us to *be* at this time of year?

How does he want us to live today? What are *his* priorities, *his* ideas about the things we are concerned about, *his* values – *his* will?

At the start of these notes, let's shift our focus, if we can. With Moses, let's say: 'I want to find out what the Lord says about this. And that might mean a wait.' God will speak if we give him the time – even during Advent!

Lord, help me to give you time and space even in this, the busiest time of the year. Help me to hear your voice today. Amen

SHEILA JACOBS

Seek – you'll find

'Then you will call on me and come and pray to me, and I will listen to you. You will seek me and find me when you seek me with all your heart. I will be found by you,' declares the Lord. (NIV)

God actually gives us a promise here about seeking him – which often entails, in my experience, quite a lot of waiting. When we seek him out, he tells us that we will certainly meet with him.

What does it mean to meet with the living God? Do we all have to run into a desert, as Elijah did in 1 Kings 19, to encounter that 'gentle whisper'? While the wilderness place in our lives can be a doorway to meeting with God, it is not the only way.

It seems here that God is saying that we need to seek him wholeheartedly, not in the haphazard way I often do. In other words, we have to mean it – we must be sincere.

The run-up to Christmas can be stressful for some and fun for others. But for many, it's a difficult time which can begin with a growing dread sometime in November. There are people (and it may be you, or someone you know) who don't enjoy the season at all. Perhaps it's the empty place at the table or the loneliness of having no one special to spend the celebrations with.

I admit I don't particularly enjoy Christmas. A couple of years ago, I resolved to make it all about Jesus – to look for him among the trinkets and baubles and glitter of this time of year. Yes, I had to wait for him – indeed, I was waiting for the Messiah to arrive. I lit an Advent candle, spending time in silence. And he spoke words of comfort to me, which helped me change my view of Christmases past and present. Hopefully, this will also impact the future.

When we seek him, we'll find him, even if sometimes we have to wait. And that's a promise.

Do you find it easy to wait on God? Or not? Does it help you to know that there is a promise attached for those who seek after him?

SHEILA JACOBS

Waiting expectantly

In the morning, Lord, you hear my voice; in the morning I lay my requests before you and wait expectantly. (NIV)

The psalms are full of people remembering God, recalling his goodness, crying out and seeking his face. Here, we see the shepherd-boy-turned-king, David, expressing something that is massively important – the expectancy of hearing from God.

Yesterday we looked at the promise of God for those who seek him – that he would be found by them. Here we find that David, who had an intimate relationship with God, *expected* to encounter him.

Waiting on God can be a lengthy process – although not always. He may speak in ways we don't expect and the answer he gives or brings may not be quite to our liking. But the fact is, God is not silent. He will speak if we give him the space to do so. I talk a lot. I'm trying to listen more. I talk a lot *at* God and sometimes don't wait for an answer. If I treated my friends like that, I'm fairly sure they wouldn't like it.

But what about the times God doesn't seem to notice us? We may have been trying to hear him on a specific issue for some time. But there's – well – nothing.

No one said waiting would be easy. We may have a tendency to give up, even though we have a feeling that God would speak if we gave him a little more time.

As we wait for the coming Saviour, we know he will arrive. At Christmas we celebrate his first coming. But there will be a time when he will come again – not as a baby, but as a conquering king. Are we ready for that time? Are we waiting patiently, expectantly? Or have doubts crept in: 'It's been so long…'? Are you expectant today?

Are you able to pray and wait in expectancy? Or are you tired of waiting? Spend some time reflecting on how God may, indeed, have answered you. Have you missed his quiet voice?

SHEILA JACOBS

Waiting in hope

We wait in hope for the Lord; he is our help and our shield. In him our hearts rejoice, for we trust in his holy name. (NIV)

When the world was hit by the coronavirus, I was struck by two things about my faith: how far I had moved away from intimacy with God – which I had known during the isolation I experienced for so many years through agoraphobia – and how the only help, the only shield, the only hope we have is in God.

It is so easy to move away from God, even though we aren't aware of it. I was doing Christian stuff, but my heart was actually quite a long way away from the Lord. I realised, repented and, after a while, began to be reminded of his peaceful presence. But it took time! Social isolation when you're living alone, as many of you may know, is not at all easy – whatever the reason. As a friend of mine pointed out, there are many people who perpetually live in virtual lockdown due to disability and illness.

In a time of enforced waiting, we need to make sure we aren't waiting in fear, but waiting in hope for the Lord, our help, our shield. You may be in a situation where you need to kick-start your hope and trust in God. Whatever is happening in your world, remember the one we can trust. We can wait in hope because of who he is.

During the first Advent, it is as if the world was waiting – waiting for the Messiah to be born. I am sure the hundreds of years of God's silence between the Old and New Testaments tested the patience of his people. Let's make sure we don't lose hope in whatever we are waiting for from God; let your heart rejoice today as you think about Jesus coming into the world to save us, to bless us and to restore us.

Whatever your circumstances, remember that the Lord is God. Think on him and rejoice in the fact that this is your God, your Saviour and friend.

SHEILA JACOBS

The blessing of waiting

Yet the Lord longs to be gracious to you; therefore he will rise up to show you compassion. For the Lord is a God of justice. Blessed are all who wait for him! (NIV)

Those who wait for God are blessed. What a wonderful promise!

In context, we can see that God 'longs' to be gracious to a people who are wildly disobedient. But God is compassionate. He desires to shower his love and blessings on us!

I have long thought that being in relationship with God isn't really about telling him what I want and expecting him to bless that, but about asking him what he wants and joining in. I find it so easy, though, to wander off and do my own thing. I've found myself encountering dead ends because of that.

What does it mean to be blessed by God? We're told here that we're blessed if we 'wait for him'. So I suppose that doesn't necessarily mean that blessings are of the material sort: the big house, the Ferrari, the horse, the smart furniture, the (fill in the blanks). The blessing of his presence far surpasses it all.

Waiting for him, waiting for encounter, waiting for that touch from the Lord – nothing is better than hearing his voice and knowing it's him.

During the Advent season, the season of waiting, we're focused on that greatest blessing: that God sent his Son to reconcile us to himself, to restore broken relationships and to give us hope of eternal life.

This world can bring many blessings. They can be real and wonderful, but superficial and shallow too. However we are blessed, let's thank the Lord – but keep a genuine perspective on what's important. Let's keep in mind that waiting on the Lord brings true blessing.

Blessings can often surprise you – they can turn up in all sorts of ways. But the real treasure is found in a manger, in a dirty stable on Christmas Day.

Think of five things the Lord has blessed you with this week. How do they compare with the blessing of encountering God?

SHEILA JACOBS

The blessing of strength

But those who hope in the Lord will renew their strength. They will soar on wings like eagles; they will run and not grow weary, they will walk and not be faint. (NIV)

During the time of the coronavirus lockdown, I had a dream. I was in my living room and someone had rearranged the furniture. My bureau was blocking the door. I felt as if someone would come and put it back into order – at the right time. Then I felt the Lord saying that he was the one who was ultimately in charge. I had a further impression that he was telling me to switch the torch on. It dawned on me that I needed to shine the light of hope into what was a difficult and dark situation.

I found myself encouraged by the thought that God was, indeed, sovereign. That I had to look up and beyond the immediate circumstances and know that God was still on the throne, working his purposes out. The situation was known to him. Nothing took him by surprise. My hope was renewed: like the apostle Paul in Philippians 1:13, I could look beyond the 'chains' and know that God would work everything out for the good. Like the eagle, I could soar in that understanding.

As Christmas draws ever closer, what a time to remember that God has a plan. We couldn't save ourselves, so he sent a rescuer to redeem and restore us, even before we knew we needed help.

You might find Christmas stressful, difficult and financially challenging; you might be enjoying the excitement and the thought of seeing family and friends, parties and celebrations. But however you're coping with the run-up to the festive season, remember that there's one who rewards hope with renewed strength. There is something about lifting our eyes to Jesus that brings a flash of joy to the heart as we realise what he has come to do. Now that really is worth celebrating.

Do you need to ask the Lord to renew your strength today? Put your hope in him. He loves you – he came to save you!

SHEILA JACOBS

The blessing of good

I say to myself, 'The Lord… I will wait for him.' The Lord is good to those whose hope is in him, to the one who seeks him; it is good to wait quietly. (NIV)

Another promise from the Lord for those who wait is found in this passage in Lamentations. The Lord is *good* to the people who put their hope in him, so we can wait for him expecting his goodness.

Christmas is a great time to remember the good things God has done. The best thing, of course, is the love he lavished upon us in sending his Son to remove the separation of sin, so that we could be restored to relationship with our heavenly Father. Psalm 34:8 tells us: 'Taste and see that the Lord is good; blessed is the one who takes refuge in him.' God is good!

The trouble is, sometimes we don't believe it. Maybe we were brought up in a household that didn't express a belief in a God who was loving goodness. The concept of a good Father can be difficult to grasp for those who haven't experienced any kind of goodness in a human father. But we need to explore the character and nature of God, to draw our own conclusions about who he really is.

We only get to know people when we invest our time in them. We can know a lot *about* a person without being in their company, but it's only as we spend time with them that we truly come to know them (and then, perhaps, to trust them). Likewise, as we spend time with God, we will become familiar with who he is.

Although this is such a busy time of year, I encourage you to spend a few minutes each day simply being still and remembering how much God loves *you*. As you wait quietly, patiently, invite the Holy Spirit to come so that you can experience the goodness of God.

Holy Spirit, please come and reveal your heart to me today. Help me to encounter God and to know your love and peace in the midst of this busy day. Amen

SHEILA JACOBS

Waiting for the gift

On one occasion, while he was eating with them, he gave them this command: 'Do not leave Jerusalem, but wait for the gift my Father promised, which you have heard me speak about.' (NIV)

The New Testament tells us that after Jesus died and rose again, he commanded his disciples to *wait* for the gift that was promised. This gift, of course, was the Holy Spirit.

We may not feel as if there is much sitting around and waiting at this time of year, and yet it is a time of waiting: to see family and friends; to celebrate together; and yes, to receive gifts!

The gift Jesus was speaking about had already been promised during his upper-room discourse. The Holy Spirit would come and would empower the waiting disciples to live for their God. We can't do this Christian life alone. The only one who can live a life pleasing to God is God himself: and he puts his life into us, so we can live for him.

At Christmas we remember the coming of the King, but we must also keep our eyes on the rest of the story. He died to pay the price for our sins. He rose again because death had no hold on him. He promised to send us 'another advocate' who would help us, be with us forever and would 'be in' us (John 14:16–17).

What a sense of anticipation the first disciples must have had, waiting for a promise like this: they had no idea what the gift would be like – but of course, God's gifts are good.

Maybe you are waiting for something other than Christmas this year. Perhaps you feel God has made you a promise of some sort, but it hasn't happened yet. Remember, if he has promised, he will fulfil it – in his own time. How does it make you feel to think that God is waiting with you?

Have you ever waited on God for a fresh infilling of his Spirit?

SHEILA JACOBS

Waiting eagerly

We ourselves, who have the first fruits of the Spirit, groan inwardly as we wait eagerly for our adoption to sonship, the redemption of our bodies. (NIV)

I love being a day chaplain in a retreat house. Sometimes I wake up early on 'chaplain day', eagerly anticipating the people I'll meet and what God might do. But waiting eagerly for the fullness of what Jesus has bought for me: that really is awesome.

We know, of course, that Christmas isn't just about angels and shepherds and twinkling lights. It's about God who became man and made it possible for us to be adopted into God's family, as sons and daughters.

You may have grown up enjoying a wonderful family life and Christmas means meeting with people you love. Or, conversely, you may not have had such a great upbringing: perhaps you felt your family let you down in some way or you felt rejected. Maybe you feel your church family has let you down, too. Unresolved hurt and disappointment can sadly bring alienation from other believers – our brothers and sisters in Christ.

But because Jesus came to earth that very first Christmas, we never have to feel rejected again. We *belong*. We are *wanted*. And it isn't just for now – it's for eternity. So let's try to see from that amazing perspective, so we can let go of any hurt and rejection, and focus on acceptance and love, forgiveness and restoration, as we anticipate our beautiful future.

If you are feeling alone, read today's passage again. Anyone who comes to Jesus will find an eternal home, starting now. The kingdom of God is about 'now and not yet'. One day, as we wait for the promise of God to be fulfilled, we'll know a different kind of life, with no suffering or disappointment – indeed, nothing will get in the way of enjoying the perfection of who God our Father is, forever.

Are you waiting eagerly for the fulfilment of your adoption into God's family? Do you get excited about the fact that if you know Jesus, you are a child of God?

SHEILA JACOBS

Radical promise

The angel answered, 'The Holy Spirit will come on you, and the power of the Most High will overshadow you…' 'I am the Lord's servant,' Mary answered. 'May your word to me be fulfilled.' Then the angel left her. (NIV)

As we come closer to Christmas Day, the conversation between Mary and her heavenly visitor is worth considering.

God makes a unique promise to Mary. And she doesn't seem to doubt that God's word will come to pass. In a society that hardly looked kindly upon young, pregnant, unmarried mothers, she takes a radical step of obedience. She cannot know that her fiancé will believe her or still want to marry her. It's a remarkable picture of faith. But she says to the angel: 'May your word to me be fulfilled.' I wonder if we can say the same in our own situations.

It's hard to let go of our own wants and desires, isn't it? Many times, I have been aware of the 'shopping list' nature of my prayers, but God is not some kind of cosmic slot machine. If I say these words properly, if I do this or that, then he is obligated to do what I want – no! That's reducing God to something I have created in my own image. A god who works for *me*.

It's often the big challenges of life that shake us out of our complacency and show us plainly our need to lean wholly on someone far stronger than ourselves; to re-evaluate our relationship with God. We may think we're in control of our lives, but actually, circumstances can prove that we're not. Realising this may stir us to come again in humility to the one who is sovereign, surrendering ourselves to his will for our lives, waiting for his promise to us to be revealed and then fulfilled. And that wait might be difficult, uncomfortable or even painful.

You simply can't hurry a birth. You have to wait. But some things grow in the waiting.

What do you think the Lord might be growing in you as you wait for him? Spend some time thanking him for the unseen ways he is working in your life.

SHEILA JACOBS

Even if you don't see it...

Joseph… did what the angel of the Lord had commanded him and took Mary home as his wife. But he did not consummate their marriage until she gave birth to a son. And he gave him the name Jesus. (NIV)

What an amazing character Joseph is! If ever there was a man who exuded patience, it was this man. His fiancée is pregnant, and he knows the child isn't his; then he receives a heavenly explanation and waits alongside his bride for the Saviour to be born.

We cannot know for sure when Joseph died, but from the biblical narrative it seems plain that he was no longer alive during Jesus' ministry. So he probably didn't see any of the signs, wonders and miracles that marked Jesus out as the promised Messiah.

Joseph does not seem to doubt the heavenly messenger. It's as if he wakes up from the dream and says, 'Okay, right, that's fine, let's do it.' He was a man awaiting a promise – a promise of the one who would come (see Isaiah 53) – and when he was told that promise would be fulfilled in his wife's child, he accepted it. But he probably didn't see the fulfilment in his lifetime. Perhaps he just knew his eldest son as a (very good) carpenter!

What do we do when we feel we have been waiting for God to move or act in a certain situation and he doesn't seem to be doing anything? Dare we believe that the promise may be fulfilled at some future point, but that we won't be around to see it? And are we okay with that?

We all have our individual hopes, dreams and ambitions. I wonder how easy it is, sometimes, to lay those down and trust God with the timing. Faithfully praying and waiting is difficult when you don't see any results. But just as we cannot see a seed growing underground, it doesn't mean that God is not working.

Is there a person (or people) you have been praying for to know Jesus for a long time? Thank God that he has heard your prayers. Can you trust him with the outcome?

SHEILA JACOBS

It's for you!

And there were shepherds living out in the fields near by, keeping watch over their flocks at night. An angel of the Lord appeared to them, and the glory of the Lord shone around them. (NIV)

In New Testament times, shepherds were not considered desirable company. And yet the exciting thing about the Christmas story is that God chose them to be among the first to meet his Son. God meets with the outcasts and invites them to the party. Interesting, isn't it, that he hasn't changed? He does the same today.

I wonder what the shepherds were doing when they were on that hillside before the angel turned up? I suspect they were probably half-asleep, thinking about – well – sheep, supper, how their kids were getting along at home… all the usual stuff of life. I somehow doubt they were thinking great spiritual thoughts (although they might have been, who knows?). Then there's a heavenly visitation, they meet Jesus and their world is turned upside down.

Jesus does tend to do that, doesn't he? Breaking into the quietness of our lives and inviting us on a great adventure. It doesn't matter who you are, what you've done or where you've been. He's got a plan for you.

The shepherds would have been waiting for their Messiah as much as anyone. But I wonder what they thought he'd be like. Did they ever believe God and his Messiah would be interested in 'mere' shepherds? Acts 2:39 says: 'The promise is for you and your children and for all who are far off – for all whom the Lord our God will call.' Forgiveness and infilling with the Spirit of God: a promise that is for everyone.

Perhaps you have been longing to know the promised Messiah but have delayed responding to him for some reason. Maybe you think his call is not for you. But it is. Why not come to him now, like the shepherds, that very first Christmas?

Sing or play a carol – something like 'Joy to the World'. Isn't it wonderful that Jesus has come to give a fresh start to all who would welcome him? Praise God today!

SHEILA JACOBS

Keeping focused

'Sovereign Lord, as you have promised, you may now dismiss your servant in peace. For my eyes have seen your salvation.' (NIV)

Now here is someone who has been waiting a long time for the promise of God – and who ultimately sees that promise in the face of a child!

I love Simeon's outburst of praise in verses 29 to 32. How long he'd been waiting; and now he could depart, knowing that God had been faithful to his promise. It's wonderful when we see God move, especially after a long period of waiting. How our faith is raised in that moment!

The apostle Paul worked ardently with the burgeoning church. We can read something of his joy when he saw good things happening in 1 Thessalonians 1:8–10, which concludes that the people 'turned to God from idols to serve the living and true God, and to wait for his Son from heaven, whom he raised from the dead' – Jesus: the rescuer.

It isn't easy to keep your eyes on Jesus – and not just at this increasingly busy time of year! Clearly, Simeon never took his eyes off the ball and was rewarded. Let's make sure that we do the same, even when it's so easy to cram our lives full of everything else.

I have often thought that the broad, primrose-laden walkway is an enticing alternative to the rather narrow, rocky path I sometimes have to tread as a Christian. But when I remember where that walkway leads, it becomes easier to avert my eyes from the broad road. That road leads nowhere good; the narrow path leads somewhere beautiful (Matthew 7:13). It's about keeping focused.

Just as Simeon waited and was rewarded, and Paul's people were waiting for someone beyond this earth, let's remember, amid the hustle and the bustle, the turkey and the trimmings and the frantic last-minute gift-wrapping, that there's a greater reality – and we belong to it.

How can you spend five (or more!) minutes alone with the Lord every day over Christmas to rest and to wait in his presence? Think about it.

SHEILA JACOBS

Encountering the King

There was also a prophet, Anna… She was very old… She never left the temple but worshipped night and day, fasting and praying… She gave thanks to God and spoke about the child to all. (NIV)

Age is no barrier to evangelism! On this, the day we celebrate Jesus' birthday, many of us meeting with relatives old and young, we remember that a grandmother figure who had been worshipping, 'fasting and praying', was gifted with meeting the Saviour face to face. Surely God was good to Anna, who waited on him 'night and day'.

As we have been considering, waiting on God isn't easy, and sometimes we may not be sure what it is we are actually waiting for; perhaps it's for a specific answer to prayer, fulfilment of a vision for our life or someone else's. I wonder, though, how our lives might change if we just waited on *him* for *his* sake. Because waiting on God surely brings a specific reward: his presence.

Times of rest and solitude – whether we have chosen them or not – can help us slow down and remember that all things pass. We are on a pilgrimage, after all, and our ultimate destination is not *here*. How often I forget that there is a bigger picture to consider. I need to fix my eyes on what is eternal, while not leaving the things I need to do in this world undone.

A Saviour came from heaven to earth. Anna, who had spent years in his presence, recognised him and joyfully told everyone the good news. He's here. He has come. And we can meet with him.

I don't know how you feel about Christmas, but I hope these notes have encouraged you to spend time with the one who loves you best, to consider his promises for those who wait on him and to receive your reward as you encounter the King. Happy Christmas!

Father, words cannot express my thanks for your Son. You are good to those who wait on you. Like Anna, help me to recognise you, whatever life brings today and in the days to come. Amen

SHEILA JACOBS

Psalm 30: looking back and forwards

Maxine Hallett writes:

I think Psalm 30 is a powerful psalm. Clearly David had been in a dark, bad place, perhaps suffering ill health. He was out of his depth and had taken his eyes off the Lord but, after much prayer and petition, he experiences God's rescue and is truly joyous in giving God all the glory.

I can identify with David, because I too have been out of my depth. As a young adult, my life was spiralling out of control because of bad choices I had made. I was addicted to drugs and completely lost until I met the Lord and he rescued me. Life did not change overnight, but it certainly started to get a lot better when I put God in the centre of my life. Now, like David, I can look back and see how much God has been working over the years to help me become the person that I am today.

I believe this psalm has many lessons for us, not least the importance of praising the Lord when he has brought us through difficult seasons in our lives. We should never take this for granted but thank our Father and give him all the glory. It also warns us against complacency and encourages us to look to God in all circumstances.

The occasion of this psalm was a celebration. Some commentators say it was for the dedication of the temple, which David prepared for and his son Solomon built. Others suggest it was written for the dedication of David's palace or perhaps referred to the tent which temporarily housed the Ark of the Covenant, which David had brought back to Jerusalem. Whatever the occasion, David clearly wanted to put the focus on God and to remember what God had done for him.

As we look forward to celebrating a new year, I want to encourage you to read through this psalm slowly, thinking back over the last year. How has God been working in your life? What has he been teaching you? What challenges have you faced? What do you want to thank him for or say sorry for?

Let's learn from David as he looks back on his experiences and commit to keeping our eyes focused on God for the year ahead.

The importance of praise

I will exalt you, Lord, for you rescued me. (NLT)

David's opening words challenge me. He says that he will 'exalt' the Lord, which means to glorify, acclaim, raise up, magnify, honour. Do I do that enough? David nearly always begins his psalms with words of praise and thanksgiving; indeed, praise is mentioned over 130 times throughout the psalms. Even as David handed over his kingdom and the building of the temple to his son Solomon, he led the people in a song of praise, reminding them of God's goodness and generosity (1 Chronicles 29:10–20).

One of my close friends is a worship leader and she uses the term 'worth-ship', saying worship is anything that declares God's worth. When we come to God in praise, we take our eyes off ourselves and focus instead on him and his attributes.

Like David, we can begin with thanksgiving, which is the gateway to praise. I have taken this on board in my daily prayers, and each evening I give thanks and praise for three things that have happened during the day. Sometimes it's three things that have got me through the day! I have found this to be a really helpful discipline, as it encourages me to focus on God first before I bring my concerns to him. Now I make a point of jotting down 'God moments' in my journal, and I am constantly amazed and encouraged by God's goodness to me.

Many Christians have testified to the power of praise. It can strengthen our resolve and build our faith. Scripture teaches us to 'praise the Lord at all times' (Psalm 34:1) and to 'be thankful in all circumstances' (1 Thessalonians 5:18).

Let's start today to thank God for his goodness to us and make praise and thanksgiving a priority for the year ahead.

Dear Lord, our Father, daily you show us love, mercy and forgiveness. Your goodness is overflowing and your faithfulness knows no boundaries. For these and so much more, Lord, we thank you. Amen

MAXINE HALLETT

Know you are not alone

You brought me up from the grave, O Lord. You kept me from falling into the pit of death (NLT)

For many years I have co-led groups of women on the Recovery Course (for people struggling with addictions) and witnessed lives being transformed. When they arrive, these women look dishevelled and downcast. After a few weeks, they realise they are not being judged for poor choices made and they can seek forgiveness. By the end of the course, they are gleaming, full of confidence and joy, their lives restored by the love of God. With Jesus firmly set in their hearts, they have a new life, built upon his firm foundations. To witness their transformation is breathtaking.

It is unclear whether David had been physically ill or under spiritual attack when he wrote his psalm, but we get a real sense in these first few verses that he had been on a rollercoaster ride through lamentation to joy. We can sense his relief as God answers his prayer and rescues him from despair. His life has been restored.

What challenges are you facing as we move into a new year? Perhaps you are struggling because you do not enjoy your job, or maybe you are unemployed and despair of finding a new role. Perhaps it is a relationship with a friend or loved one that is starting to trouble you, or a health concern that is wearing you down.

When we focus our attention on God and call out to him, we are carried in his strong arms to safety. It may feel that we are all alone in our pit, but we are not. Reach out, call his name, God is waiting! His love is the firm foundation that we need to feel under our feet.

Sit quietly in the Lord's presence. Remind yourself of his love and his transforming power, and then bring to him your concerns for yourself or for others.

MAXINE HALLETT

Anger management

*For his anger lasts only a moment, but his favour lasts a lifetime!
Weeping may last through the night, but joy comes with the morning.
(NLT)*

Have you ever gone to bed on an argument? Perhaps you said some cross
words to a family member or friend on the phone and were disconnected,
or had the door slammed shut before having a chance to clear the air? As
a parent, I have spent many years feeling that it was important for me to
get the last word in – a challenge with teenagers!

David is clear here that God may get angry from time to time because
of the way humans act, but he doesn't stay angry. 'His anger lasts only a
moment.' This really challenged me to think about how I react to situations
and I wanted to learn from David's words.

I began to ask myself, 'How would Jesus act in this situation?' I tried to
look at things through the eyes of the Lord and ask what I could do differently. Now I no longer need to get the last word in. When I feel angry, I try
to pause and seek God's wisdom. Sometimes I realise that saying nothing is the way forward. On other occasions, I recognise that I need to say
sorry for overreacting. Taking some time to reflect brings calm and defuses
the situation. The day ends on a sweeter note and I thank the Lord for his
guidance.

Some circumstances may need more prayer and advice, but generally
I find things look better after a good night's sleep.

Maybe you are holding on to a harsh word said to you by somebody
in anger, or feeling guilty because of something you said in anger. Take it
to the Lord and hold on to the words that 'weeping may last through the
night, but joy comes with the morning'.

---

*Thank you, Lord, that you are slow to anger and quick to show us love. Teach
us how to be the same. Amen*

MAXINE HALLETT

The challenge of the good times

When I was prosperous, I said, 'Nothing can stop me now!' Your favour, O Lord, made me as secure as a mountain. Then you turned away from me, and I was shattered. (NLT)

David made plenty of mistakes during his reign, and I find it reassuring to know that even those who found favour with God could still make bad choices.

Here David recognises that he had begun to take things for granted, to put his trust in his wealth and his own strength, forgetting that his status and security came from God. For a while, things were fine, but then he realised God was no longer with him and things began to fall apart.

I think there is a real challenge for us here. We are quick to turn to God when we are distressed, seeking his guidance and direction, but what about when things are going well? Do we still seek God or do we become complacent, find new priorities and forget to be thankful for God's blessings? We might even feel entitled to our good fortune and take the credit for ourselves, instead of recognising God as our provider.

Proverbs 16:18 warns: 'Pride goes before destruction, a haughty spirit before a fall' (NIV). It is a long way down from the top of a mountain back to the valley! But, as we come tumbling down, we can cry out to God for mercy, as David did, and know his forgiveness.

Like David, we learn that we cannot do life on our own; it just does not work! We need to keep our focus on God regardless of the situation we find ourselves in, good or bad.

A friend of mine told me once he was a FROG – Fully Reliant On God – or that he tried to be. How about that for a New Year's resolution?

Lord, forgive us when we take your goodness for granted and become complacent. Thank you that you carry us in your heart even when we have taken our eyes off you, and that you are always ready to welcome us home. Amen
MAXINE HALLETT

From sorrow to dancing

You did it: you changed wild lament into whirling dance; You ripped off my black mourning band and decked me with wildflowers. (MSG)

The winter months can feel long and drawn out. My teenage daughter has a horse, so we are out in all weathers and the winter can be especially hard. On the shortest day of the year, we always feel joyful and give praise to the Lord for the changing seasons. We know that from that point, every day going forward will start to get a little lighter, and soon we will witness the first signs of spring as crocuses and snowdrops start to appear.

Life, too, has its different seasons and, in this verse, David is remembering all the times God has brought him from sadness to joy. I wonder if he was thinking about how God rescued him and protected him when Saul was hunting him and tried to kill him (1 Samuel 19—31), or perhaps he was thinking about the times he sinned and his experiences of God's forgiveness and mercy.

I love the exuberance of this verse and the idea that things can change in an instant. 'You did it!' says David, 'you ripped off my black mourning band.' Whatever situation David is thinking about, God acted decisively and completely changed things around.

But sometimes we have to wait a while and, like the winter months, our laments, uncertainty or challenges seem to go on and on. In this case, we need to look for the glimmers of joy that God brings to us in our sadness. It could be a word of scripture that jumps off the page, a kind word from a friend or a walk among trees and flowers that lifts our spirits. In what ways has God led you from sadness to joy this year?

Open our eyes, Lord, as we journey through different seasons with you. Fill us with your Holy Spirit as you wrap your powerful hands around ours and encourage us to dance. Amen

MAXINE HALLETT

Share God's love with others

I'm about to burst with song; I can't keep quiet about you. God, my God, I can't thank you enough. (MSG)

David can't contain his joy as he recalls God's goodness and mercy, and how God has answered his prayers. Now he wants to tell the whole world how wonderful God is. When I read this verse, it makes me want to burst with joy and recount all the times that God has been working in my life.

I am fortunate to live close to wonderful countryside and woodland, and love going out for walks with my dog. I can really switch off and enjoy a powerful sense of God's presence as he walks with me. Like David, I am often overwhelmed with joy as God awakens my soul and I want to share that joy with others.

Keen to share God's blessings, I began to take photographs on my walks and I use these in my work with the seniors at my local church. Many of these elderly people have limited mobility, so they enjoy sharing all the wonderful things I have seen, as well as hearing what I am learning about God. I am truly thankful for these opportunities and for the life that I now enjoy.

What about you? Where do you feel closest to God? What opportunities do you have to share God's goodness and love? Let us not keep quiet about knowing God but seek to pass on his love to others in 2022. This might be through helping out in our community, looking out for our neighbours or simply sharing a smile and a kind word with those we meet.

Life may bring its ups and downs, but we can be people of joy as we focus on God's care, provision and patience with us, always giving thanks to him for everything he does for us.

Father, thank you for the ways you have been working in my life this year. Help me to share the joy of knowing you with others and to embrace every new day with thankfulness and praise. Amen

MAXINE HALLETT

Recommended reading

Celebrating Christmas
Embracing joy through art and reflections
Reflections by Amy Boucher Pye
Illustrations by Leo Boucher
978 1 80039 051 5 £8.99
brfonline.org.uk

Considering not only the story of Mary and Joseph journeying to Bethlehem, where Jesus was born, but also our modern-day expressions of Christmas, they bring light and life to what can be a fraught and exhausting season. A book perfect for giving as a gift or using oneself to foster joy and peace.

The BRF Book of 365 Bible Reflections
with contributions from BRF authors, supporters and well-wishers
978 1 80039 100 0 £14.99
brfonline.org.uk

The Bible is at the heart of BRF's work, and this special anniversary collection is a celebration of the Bible for BRF's centenary year. Bringing together a fantastically wide-ranging writing team of authors, supporters and well-wishers from all areas of BRF's work, this resource is designed to help us go deeper into the story of the Bible and reflect on how we can share it in our everyday lives. Including sections which lead us through the Bible narrative as well as thematic and seasonal sections, it is the perfect daily companion to resource your spiritual journey.

To order

Online: **brfonline.org.uk**
Telephone: +44 (0)1865 319700
Mon–Fri 9.30–17.00

Delivery times within the UK are normally 15 working days. Prices are correct at the time of going to press but may change without prior notice.

Title	Price	Qty	Total
Celebrating Christmas	£8.99		
The BRF Book of 365 Bible Reflections	£14.99		

POSTAGE AND PACKING CHARGES			
Order value	UK	Europe	Rest of world
Under £7.00	£2.00		
£7.00–£29.99	£3.00	Available on request	Available on request
£30.00 and over	FREE		

Total value of books	
Donation	
Postage and packing	
Total for this order	

Please complete in BLOCK CAPITALS

Title _____ First name/initials _____ Surname_____

Address_____

_____ Postcode _____

Acc. No. _____ Telephone _____

Email_____

Method of payment

☐ Cheque (made payable to BRF)   ☐ MasterCard / Visa credit / Visa debit

Card no. ☐☐☐☐ ☐☐☐☐ ☐☐☐☐ ☐☐☐☐

Expires end ☐☐ M M ☐☐ Y Y   Security code* ☐☐☐   Last 3 digits on the reverse of the card

Signature* _____ Date _____ /_____ /_____

*ESSENTIAL IN ORDER TO PROCESS YOUR ORDER

Registered with FUNDRAISING REGULATOR

Please return this form to:

BRF, 15 The Chambers, Vineyard, Abingdon OX14 3FE | **enquiries@brf.org.uk**
To read our terms and find out about cancelling your order, please visit **brfonline.org.uk/terms**.

The Bible Reading Fellowship (BRF) is a Registered Charity (233280)

Each issue of *Day by Day with God* is available from Christian bookshops everywhere. Copies may also be available through your church book agent or from the person who distributes Bible reading notes in your church.

Alternatively you may obtain *Day by Day with God* on subscription direct from the publishers. There are two kinds of subscription:

Individual subscriptions
covering 3 issues for 4 copies or less, payable in advance
(including postage & packing).

To order, please complete the details on page 144 and return with the appropriate payment to: BRF, 15 The Chambers, Vineyard, Abingdon OX14 3FE

You can also use the form on page 144 to order a gift subscription for a friend.

Group subscriptions
covering 3 issues for 5 copies or more, sent to one UK address (post free).

Please note that the annual billing period for group subscriptions runs from 1 May to 30 April.

To order, please complete the details on page 143 and return with the appropriate payment to: BRF, 15 The Chambers, Vineyard, Abingdon OX14 3FE

You will receive an invoice with the first issue of notes.

All our Bible reading notes can be ordered online by visiting
brfonline.org.uk/collections/subscriptions

Day by Day with God is also available as
an app for Android, iPhone and iPad
brfonline.org.uk/collections/apps

Follow us on Instagram: **@daybydaywithgod**

All subscription enquiries should be directed to:
BRF, 15 The Chambers, Vineyard, Abingdon OX14 3FE
+44 (0)1865 319700 | **enquiries@brf.org.uk**

DAY BY DAY WITH GOD GROUP SUBSCRIPTION FORM

All our Bible reading notes can be ordered online by visiting
brfonline.org.uk/collections/subscriptions

The group subscription rate for *Day by Day with God* will be £14.25 per person until April 2022.

☐ I would like to take out a group subscription for .... (quantity) copies.

☐ Please start my order with the January 2022 / May 2022 / September 2022* issue. I would like to pay annually/receive an invoice* with each edition of the notes. (*delete as appropriate)

Please do not send any money with your order. Send your order to BRF and we will send you an invoice.

Name and address of the person organising the group subscription:

Title .... First name/initials .... Surname ....

Address ....

.... Postcode ....

Telephone .... Email ....

Church ....

Name and address of the person paying the invoice if the invoice needs to be sent directly to them:

Title .... First name/initials .... Surname ....

Address ....

.... Postcode ....

Telephone .... Email ....

Please return this form to:
BRF, 15 The Chambers, Vineyard, Abingdon OX14 3FE | enquiries@brf.org.uk

To read our terms and find out about cancelling your order,
please visit **brfonline.org.uk/terms**.

The Bible Reading Fellowship is a Registered Charity (233280)

DAY BY DAY WITH GOD INDIVIDUAL/GIFT SUBSCRIPTION FORM

To order online, please visit **brfonline.org.uk/collections/subscriptions**

- ☐ I would like to give a gift subscription (please provide both names and addresses)
- ☐ I would like to take out a subscription myself (complete your name and address details only once)

Title _____ First name/initials _____ Surname _____

Address _____

_____ Postcode _____

Telephone _____ Email _____

Gift subscription name _____

Gift subscription address _____

_____ Postcode _____

Gift subscription (20 words max. or include your own gift card):

_____

_____

Please send *Day by Day with God* beginning with the January 2022 / May 2022 / September 2022 issue (*delete as appropriate*):

(please tick box)	UK	Europe	Rest of world
1-year subscription	☐ 18.00	☐ £25.95	☐ £29.85
2-year subscription	☐ £35.10	N/A	N/A

Optional donation to support the work of BRF £ _____

Total enclosed £ _____ (cheques should be made payable to 'BRF')

Please charge my MasterCard / Visa credit / Visa debit with £ _____

Card no. ☐☐☐☐☐ ☐☐☐☐☐ ☐☐☐☐☐ ☐☐☐☐☐

Expires end ☐☐ ☐☐   Security code* ☐☐☐   Last 3 digits on the reverse of the card

Signature* _____ Date _____/_____/_____

*ESSENTIAL IN ORDER TO PROCESS YOUR ORDER

Please return this form to:
BRF, 15 The Chambers, Vineyard, Abingdon OX14 3FE | enquiries@brf.org.uk

To read our terms and find out about cancelling your order, please visit **brfonline.org.uk/terms.** The Bible Reading Fellowship is a Registered Charity (233280)

DBDWG0321